Key Terms in Literary Theory

Also available from Continuum

Essential Guide to English Studies, Peter Childs
How to Read Texts, Neil McCaw
Literary Theory: A Guide for the Perplexed, Mary Klages
Literature, In Theory, Julian Wolfreys
Studying English Literature, edited by Ashley Chantler and
   David Higgins

Key Terms in Literary Theory

MARY KLAGES

continuum

Continuum International Publishing Group

The Tower Building	80 Maiden Lane
11 York Road	Suite 704
London SE1 7NX	New York NY 10038

www.continuumbooks.com

British Library Cataloguing-in-Publication Data
A catalogue record for this book is available from the British Library.

ISBN: HB: 978-0-8624-9190-9
PB: 978-0-8264-4267-3

Library of Congress Cataloging-in-Publication Data
Klages, Mary.
Key terms in literary theory / Mary Klages.
p. cm. – (Key terms)
Includes bibliographical references and index.
ISBN: HB: 978-0-8624-9190-9
ISBN: PB: 978-0-8264-4267-3
1. Literature–Dictionaries. 2. Criticism–Dictionaries. 3. Literature–History and criticism–Theory, etc. I. Title.
PN44.5.K58 2011
803–dc23 2011034807

Typeset by Newgen Imaging Systems Pvt Ltd, Chennai, India
Printed and bound in India

CONTENTS

Introduction: Why This Book?

Chances are, if you're reading this introduction, you already know something about literary theory; perhaps you are a student, or someone who has wondered what "literary theory" is all about and is looking for some explanations. There are lots of useful guides explaining various types of literary theory. I know, because I wrote one of them. *Literary Theory: A Guide for the Perplexed* is a comprehensive introductory guidebook to literary theory. It consists of chapters devoted to types of theories: there are essays explaining psychoanalytic theory, Marxist theory, structuralism, and postmodernism, to name a few. The book is clear and accessible; it's designed to introduce students of literature and literary theory to the basic ideas of a range of theories, and to explain those theories in ways that beginning students can grasp.

Guides like mine, however, don't yield information quickly or concisely; they are more like textbooks you read for detailed information. But this book is different. It is the one you pick up when you come across an unfamiliar term in another resource, and you want an understandable definition, or you encounter a name you don't recognize, and want to know what kind of theory he or she is associated with. It's a glossary, a dictionary, a reference book. It's a great companion to *Literary Theory: A Guide for the Perplexed*, and it's a good stand-alone volume for easy reference.

This book is divided into three sections. The first section is a glossary: an alphabetical list of "key terms" in literary theory. These are words or phrases you will very likely encounter as you become familiar with literary and cultural theory, and I do my best to explain them and place them in context.

The second section consists of biographical information about literary and cultural theorists you are likely to come across as you read different types of literary theory. All entries supply dates and a list of major works by the author, and all place each author in context. Major theorists have longer explanations, which address their theoretical projects, goals, and influences.

The third section is a bibliography, which is divided into sections. The first section lists recommended works providing an overview of various literary theories. These texts are good introductory essays. If you are just beginning to learn about literary theory, these books are excellent places to start.

The second section contains recommended anthologies of primary sources; these are collections of original essays by the various theorists. These anthologies contain the most important works of the individual theorists; they are a great resource for students who want to dive into theoretical texts.

The third section lists recommended secondary sources on particular theories and theorists; these are for more advanced study of a particular theorist or school of thought.

That's it. I hope this book is useful to you.

Key Terms and Concepts

Abjection

This term comes from the latin *ab jacto*, meaning to throw under or to move under. To be "abject" is to be subordinate and inferior, to feel an attitude of shame and worthlessness. The term is associated with Julia Kristeva's version of psychoanalysis, which focuses on the pre-Oedipal phase, when the baby is still undifferentiated from its environment and its mother's body. Abjection is the "civilized" response to anything that reminds us of the drives and desires we have thrown into the unconscious through repression during the Oedipal phase of development. The abject is what culture throws away, its garbage, or its waste products; examples of abject substances include excrement, blood (especially menstrual blood), and dead bodies. According to Kristeva, these substances recall the lack of division between self and other that characterizes the pre-Oedipal phase; they conjure the maternal body, from which the infant has to separate in order to become a self (and to create an unconscious where pre-Oedipal memories and desires are repressed). Things that are abject create a feeling of horror or disgust in the adult civilized viewer because they remind him or her of the time before differentiated selfhood; they threaten to dissolve the boundaries of the self and to return the viewer to a non-differentiated state of egolessness that is frightening to the self. Horror films and other genres that want to disturb or disrupt a sense of unity and safety use images of the abject to create this response of horror: seeing things that do not have definite boundaries, things that are shoved away from or excluded from the Western idea of order, cleanliness, and goodness, make the viewer feel queasy and uneasy, uncertain of his/her status as a unified, whole, contained self.

Absence/presence

This is one of the primary binary oppositions analysed by Jacques Derrida in *Of Grammatology*, as well as a central concept in Freudian and Lacanian psychoanalysis. The idea of "presence" refers back to a binary opposition examined by Plato, who associated speech and speaking with presence and writing with absence, since a piece of writing exists separately from its writer, who need not be present for the writing to exist or be read. Derrida argues that all systems desire "full presence," to have stability and to be able to account for everything within the system; full presence is a characteristic of the center of a system. Western metaphysics, according to Derrida, favors presence and wants to subordinate absence to it. In psychoanalytic theory, Sigmund Freud uses this preference to assert that male genitalia show the presence of the penis whereas female genitalia show the absence of the penis; this leads to castration anxiety. In Lacanian psychoanalysis, the idea of lack or absence is central to the formation of the ego or "self," which is an illusion of presence formed to relieve the anxiety of absence, which all language-using humans share. Full presence is possible only in early infancy, in the realm of the Real, where the infant does not know any separation between itself and the rest of the world; as soon as the infant enters the Imaginary, and comprehends the concept of "otherness" or separation, it experiences a fundamental lack, or absence of wholeness, which Jacques Lacan says creates our structures of desire, and which language tries, unsuccessfully, to fulfill. Language, for Lacan, is always about lack—if you did not know anything but fullness and satisfaction, you would have no need to represent thoughts in language. Only when the infant becomes aware of its existence as a being separate from that which satisfies its needs does it become aware of absence and will ever after long for a return to presence.

Alienation

As a general concept, alienation means feeling alien, foreign, or estranged to something or someone; "alienation of affection" is a legal term used to describe a situation where someone stops loving someone else. The term is employed frequently in existential philosophy and writing, to express the fundamental human alienation from paradise, or (in a psychoanalytic context) our alienation from our initial unity with the mother. Titles like *Stranger in a Strange Land* and *Invisible Man* express this sense of alienation. In Marxist theory, alienation has a more specific meaning, referring to the way that a capitalist economic system forces workers, who produce things, to feel that they do not have any rights of ownership to the things they produce. Workers are thus alienated from the products of their labor; they are also alienated from their labor itself, which becomes something they trade for money rather than something they can find satisfaction in for itself.

Anxiety

Anxiety is the psychological state that arises in infancy from the experience of separation from one's caregiver, which in classical Freudian psychoanalysis is always one's mother. At some phase in development the infant begins to become aware that the caregiver/ mother, who fulfills all needs and provides experiences of pleasure for the baby, is sometimes gone, not present to the baby's perceptions. This can also happen with any object to which the baby has a cathexis—an emotional/psychological connection charged with emotional energy (which Freud calls "libidinal energy"). The absence of the cathected object—mother's body, pacifier, one's own thumb—creates anxiety, the knowledge or awareness that the beloved object that provides comfort and satisfaction is not under the baby's control, that it can disappear.

Freud talks about anxiety in a specific context in relation to the OEDIPUS COMPLEX. He posits that when a boy first sees female genitalia, he is horrified at the absence of a penis. Since the boy in the phallic stage of development has discovered the pleasure of genital manipulation (touching his penis feels good), he has developed a cathexis to his penis. His penis becomes valuable to him, an important and perhaps irreplaceable source of pleasure. When he sees that girls do not have a penis, the boy worries that perhaps girls used to have one, just like his, but that it disappeared; this idea of separation from his penis creates anxiety, which Freud calls castration anxiety. (It is worth noting that Freud defines castration, incorrectly, as the loss of the penis, whereas in animal husbandry castration is the removal of the testicles, which renders an animal unable to produce sperm while leaving the penis intact). The boy fears the threat of separation from his beloved penis because he has castration anxiety; he represses his desire to experience pleasure from the presence of his mother's body (he has already associated the pleasurable feeling of touching his penis with the pleasurable feeling of his mother's body touching him, in nursing, in bathing, and in diaper changing) because he fears that his father, who "owns" his mother's body, will cut off his penis for wanting to have sole possession of his mother. This castration anxiety forces the boy to repress his Oedipal desires (to kill his father and have sole possession of his mother), which creates his unconscious and his superego, which is the internalized authority of the father and which will become his conscience and his sense of what is right or wrong. Freud says that castration anxiety is the primal fear that makes humans (i.e. men) become civilized—all fear of punishment is, at base, fear of castration.

For girls, of course, Freud is less clear on where castration anxiety comes from, since girls experience penis envy as soon as they know there is an anatomical distinction between the sexes. They must accept "the fact" of their castration, rather than be afraid that it might happen; the lack of castration anxiety (that the ultimate threat has already been carried out) complicates Freud's view of how a girl forms an unconscious and superego and how she resolves her own version of the Oedipus Complex.

Anxiety of influence

This is a term coined by literary critic HAROLD BLOOM, in his 1973 book of the same name, to describe the feeling that writers of one generation or era have toward their predecessors. The anxiety of influence is a fear that a writer will never be as good as one of the "greats"—for instance, that no living writer could ever be as good as Shakespeare. Bloom discusses this kind of anxiety in a psychoanalytic context, in which anxiety is a particular kind of fear generated by the OEDIPUS COMPLEX. A boy suffers castration anxiety in relation to the father, fearing that the father will cut off his penis as punishment for his sexual feelings about his mother. The anxiety of influence is modeled on castration anxiety; a writer feels inferior to his literary "fathers"—those writers who have influenced him or who have achieved what the writer wants to achieve—and feels less powerful than these fathers. Bloom took Freud's paradigm literally, conceiving of the pen as a kind of penis, and thus discussing a writer's anxiety of authorship as being akin to castration fear. SANDRA GILBERT and SUSAN GUBAR, among others, have questioned how, or whether, this concept might work for women writers, when, according to Freud, women are always already "castrated" and have therefore no reason for such anxiety.

Archaeology of knowledge

Archaeology of knowledge is a term associated with the earlier works of Michel Foucault. An archaeologist is one who uncovers and studies artifacts from the past in order to understand the culture that produced them. Foucault's archaeology examines archives not material objects: written records that reveal how a culture was able to think about a certain topic at a certain moment. The archives form what Foucault calls discourse: a set of documents from a variety of perspectives that all share a particular object and/or worldview. This worldview is what Foucault calls an episteme—the conditions that make the knowledge contained in the discursive archive possible. Foucault's work until the 1970s, influenced by structuralism and linguistics, used what he later called an "archaeological" method to examine discursive formations without paying much attention to how these discourses influenced people and social formations; his archaeology had much in common with the "history of ideas" approach that examines intellectual movements in isolation from the cultures that produced and utilized them. This method of looking at the relations among social institutions, discourses, and subjects was more than just "history" or "philosophy"; Foucault called it "archaeology" to emphasize that the process of analysing a particular social practice (such as the treatment of madness, illness, or criminal behavior) had multiple layers and dimensions, not limited to looking at structures or at how practices have changed over time.

Foucault's works that are considered "archaeological" include *Madness and Civilization, The Birth of the Clinic,* and *The Archaeology of Knowledge.*

Associative relations

As discussed by FERDINAND DE SAUSSURE in his 1916 book *Course in General Linguistics*, associative relations is one of two ways in which language is organized into a coherent structure. Words, or signs, are grouped by an individual by their associations with each other; these associations are highly subjective, and do not follow any particular rules or paradigms. An associative linguistic relation might be "baseball, pizza, cats"—these terms are connected to each other because all of them are filed in my brain under the heading "things I like." Associative relations are contrasted with SYNTAGMATIC RELATIONS, which connect words or signs on the basis of their grammatical and syntactical functions. A syntagmatic relation would be "the cat sat on the mat," where each word has a specific place and function in the sentence. Syntagmatic relations are objective and follow the structure of a particular language; associative relations are subjective and specific to an individual's way of thinking.

Base/superstructure

These two terms name the general framework for thinking about any society's cultural organization, according to Marxist thought; they describe the relationship between an economic system and the ideologies, or ways of thinking, that system produces. According to Marx, all societies are regulated and organized through their economic base, which consists of the forces and relations of production. The forces of production are the tools and methods that people use to make the things they need in order to live; forces of production might include plows and carts, for an agrarian economy, or machines, for a capitalist economy. The relations of production are the social relations that are created by and with the forces of production: an agrarian economy produces social relations of landowner and tenant, for example, while a capitalist economy produces social relations of capitalist and laborer. Together the forces and relations of production are, in Marxist theory, the economic base for all other forms of cultural activity.

Human cultures do more than produce things and relationships, however; they also produce ideas and beliefs, stories about why arrangements are organized as they are. In Marxist theory, these beliefs and stories are called "ideology"—the ideas of a culture—and are created by and through the economic base. Marx thus locates ideology as a superstructure, something that grows out of and is governed by the economic base. The superstructure contains all aspects of a culture that are not directly material, including politics, law, religion, education, and art. In classical Marxism, all elements of the superstructure can be traced back to the economic base; the mode of production (forces and relations of production) directly determines the ideologies of any society. The dominant ideas of a culture will necessarily be the ideas of the ruling class; in this argument, the content of ideologies can be changed only by changing the economic base.

Western Marxism has wrestled with this formulation throughout the twentieth century, finding the model of base/superstructure determinism to be crude and simplistic. Many Marxist theorists, starting with Friedrich Engels, have argued that cultural ideas can influence forces and relations of production; some posit that the ideological superstructure is relatively autonomous from the economic base. This is especially true in Marxist literary and cultural studies, which locate art and literature as part of the ideological superstructure; Pierre Macheray argues that tracing a direct causal relationship between an economic mode of production and a literary form is overly simplistic. An example of such a relation can be found in Soviet socialist realism, where fiction is directly informed by communist ideology; Western Marxist cultural theorists argue that such fiction is crude and unsophisticated, and that theories of ideological production must be more subtle and flexible to explain the complexity of relations between economics and artistic production.

Binary opposition

"Binary" means "two"; a binary opposition is any pair of opposites. We learn concrete opposites early in childhood: black/white, up/down, right/left, on/off, yes/no. This idea that the world is structured in terms of opposites then becomes the base on which we build more sophisticated concepts, as we come to think about good/evil, right/wrong, male/female, and so on. The binary opposition becomes the basic "unit" of our thought, both as individuals and as a culture.

The concept of binary opposition is important in structuralist thought. Anthropologist Claude Levi-Strauss, in *The Raw and the*

Cooked, said that all cultures depend upon the structure of the binary opposite; he focussed particularly at how so-called primitive cultures used the opposition "nature/culture." According to Jacques Derrida and deconstruction, binary opposition is the fundamental structure of Western philosophy and culture. Derrida argues with Levi-Strauss in his essay "Structure, Sign, and Play in the Discourse of the Human Sciences," pointing out that the nature/culture opposition contains contradictions: ideas that belong to both categories. Finding the contradictions in binary oppositions forms the basis of Derrida's deconstruction.

In binary opposition, "opposition" is the idea that the two concepts linked in the pair are mutually exclusive—they are "opposites." Black is the opposite of white, meaning that black and white cannot be the same thing. In Western philosophy, an opposite always has to be the negation of its paired term: black is what is *not* white, and white is what is*not* black. This may lead you to think about combining black and white, to come up with shades of gray. While this idea tells us about a spectrum of colors that are between black and white, no shade of gray is black *or* white; the binary opposites remain as the fixed points that cannot be merged or combined.

Another example comes from computer science. A computer is a complex system of electronic circuits, but each circuit is a simple binary unit: a circuit, like a switch, is either off or on. It cannot be both, and there is nothing in between. In mathematical terms, the switch is either 1 (on) or 0 (off); thus the code 10001001000111000 would name how a circuit operates as conducting electricity or not conducting electricity. There is nothing between 1 and 0, between on and off; the binary opposition is an absolute.

Deconstruction argues that all of Western philosophy, from the ancient Greeks through the twentieth century, has depended on this idea of an absolute binary opposition, where one thing is what it is because it is *not* its opposite. Derrida asks what would happen to the way Western culture thinks about the world if we challenged this fundamental idea of binary opposition. What if "true" was not the opposite of "false," but rather each contained elements of the other? This is the basic idea of deconstruction—what happens to ideas that are "opposites" when you remove the / (slash) between them?

A specific example might be the opposition male/female. Western culture has always insisted that each person *is* one or the other— you are either male or female, usually decided at birth on the basis of genital structure. Our pronouns, our language, our ways of dressing and decorating our bodies, our public bathrooms, laws of marriage, and almost all our political, economic, and social organizations have been built around this basic binary. You might think about how, until the twentieth century, being "female" meant being unable to vote, own property, become a doctor or lawyer.

Our social structures thus depend upon the slash between male/female being solid and dependable, and based on exclusion: one term in a binary opposition is what it is because it is not the other. Male is what is not female, and female is what is not male. But what if we could not tell the difference, or did not make all the gender distinctions that we are accustomed to? What if we dissolved the slash and male and female were relative concepts rather than absolutes? What would happen to language and bathrooms if we did not divide the world into these two opposite categories? This is the basic question that deconstruction poses. What would happen to the way we think about the world if we did not start with the basic premise of binary opposition?

Bisexuality

Bisexuality in the broadest sense refers to the sexual identity of someone who has sex with both men and women, without identifying themselves as exclusively heterosexual or homosexual. Freud's psychoanalysis posited that all humans are born bisexual, with polymorphous perverse libidinal urges directed at any person or object that creates pleasure; the mechanisms of the Oedipus and Castration Complexes are supposed to channel this original bisexuality into non-incestuous adult reproductive heterosexuality. The emergence of the gay rights movements in Western cultures in the latter half of the twentieth century brought issues of bisexuality into focus in political and academic contexts, as the binary categories of "heterosexual" and "homosexual" came under the spotlight to be questioned and deconstructed. Post-structural feminist theorist Hélène Cixous argues for a new form of bisexuality that would be liberating for men and women caught up in phallogocentric dualisms; in *The Laugh of the Medusa* (1976) she describes this "other bisexuality" in terms similar to Freud's polymorphous perversity, where sexual pleasure can come from any body or body part of any person in any combination, regardless of the biological sex or gender expression of the participants.

Bricolage

Bricolage is the French term for "do it yourself" or "odd jobs." It is used by Claude Levi-Strauss, Jacques Derrida, and by many postmodern theorists to describe the activity of using whatever materials are at hand to make something—a building, a work of art, a philosophical system—regardless of whether these materials are right, correct, or appropriate for the task at hand. Levi-Strauss describes mythmaking as bricolage, as cultures use their odds and ends of ideas and stories to create myth; Derrida contrasts bricolage with engineering or using specifically designated materials and methods to create something planned in advance according to agreed-upon rules and procedures. The person who performs an act of bricolage is a bricoleur; the person who follows plans is an engineer. Bricolage allows for greater flexibility in combining materials without regard to their original purpose, which fosters creativity and experimentation.

Capitalism

Capitalism is the term used to describe the economic mode of production that creates the social classes of owners and laborers. The inequities and inhumanity of the capitalist mode of production are the particular focus of the writings of Karl Marx, and of the social philosophies and political movements that Marx's writings have inspired. Capitalism is based on the division between those who own the means of production—the tools and resources needed to make commodities—and the proletariat, who supply the labor power to use these tools to make commodities. The laborer sells his or her labor power to the owner in exchange for a wage; the owner uses the laborer's labor power to transform raw materials, via tools, into finished goods that can be sold for profit, for more than the cost of the raw materials and the labor. The laborer adds value to the raw materials through labor, but the surplus value thus produced in the commodity belongs not to the laborer but to the owner of the means of production; this is the essence of capitalism. Laborers thus create wealth, which owners appropriate; laborers are alienated from the products of their labor and from their labor power, which becomes a commodity that laborers are required to sell in order to survive. Within this nexus of capitalism, commodities become more important than human beings, and all social relations are structured through the exchange of commodities. The private ownership of the profit produced by the surplus value created by the laborer creates and sustains class divisions, with the owners holding the power to regulate wage rates and to create and perpetuate the ruling ideologies, which protect the owners' interests. Caught between the owners and the laborers are the middle class, the bourgeoisie, who provide services to both owners and laborers; in Marx's analysis of capitalism, the bourgeoisie identify with the owning class, and thus participate in the exploitation of workers. Only the collective organized resistance of the proletariat to the system of private ownership and exploitation can end the inequities of capitalism, according to Marxist doctrine; when the workers of the world unite, they have the power to break the chains of capitalist economy and to create a new, more human, and humane system of socialism, or collective ownership of all goods and resources that are shared equally among all.

In the twentieth century, there have been many experiments with socialism and communism in an effort to defeat capitalism as the dominant global mode of production; with the collapse of the Soviet Union and the opening of China to international trade, some argue that capitalism has won the struggle.

Castration

Castration is literally the removal of the testicles from a male animal. Its significance in literary theory, however, comes from Freud's use of the term castration in psychoanalysis, where it means the removal or disappearance of the male genitals, specifically the penis. Freud posited that a boy, on first seeing a girl's genitals, will be horrified at the idea that she does not have a penis, and will think it has been cut off. The boy has associated the pleasure he gets from his penis with his desire for his mother, the original object of his libidinal drives; he has wanted to kill his father so that he can have his mother to himself. This is Freud's Oedipus Complex, which ends with the boy's fear of castration. The boy decides that the girl has had her penis cut off by the father in revenge for her desire for her mother, and becomes afraid that his father will cut off his penis for his own libidinal thoughts. This is Freud's CastrationComplex, which forces the boy to make a choice: either he risks having his penis cut off by his father, or he gives up his hope of having to himself his mother, and the pleasure her body provides, and acknowledges his father's exclusive right to his mother. The resolution of the Castration Complex results in the boy repressing his desire for his mother, which forms his unconscious, and internalizing his father's prohibition and threat of punishment, which forms his superego or conscience.

In Freudian psychoanalytic theory, castration is the ultimate fear or trauma, as a boy's narcissistic ego is invested in his penis as his primary source of pleasure. Freud bases his concept of penis envy for females on the central importance of the penis; the girl, who discovers she is already castrated, desperately wants to obtain a penis of her own to make up for her lack. In Lacanian psychoanalytic theory, the value of the penis becomes the power of the Phallus or Name of the Father, the position of full presence or completeness in the center of the Symbolic; all language-using subjects in the Symbolic are constituted by lack. Post-structural feminist theories use Freud's and Lacan's ideas of castration and lack to discuss the possibilities for a feminine language that comes more directly from the unconscious, ungoverned by the Freudian superego or the Lacanian Phallus.

Center

The center is the element that Jacques Derrida adds to Saussure's and Levi-Strauss' ideas of structure in order to talk about what keeps a structure stable. Saussure described the structure of language as a one-dimensional line; Levi-Strauss perceived the structure of myth as two-dimensional, with a horizontal axis of non-reversible time and a vertical axis of reversible time. Derrida posits that all structures, in order to be stable and unchanging, need to have a center that holds all the units of the structure in place, and that governs or limits the movements of these units. He is referring primarily to structures or systems of Western philosophy, each of which depends upon a central concept defined as the entity or power that created the system in the first place. The center is the point of origin of all the elements; the center dictates how the elements are positioned and interact within the structure. The center, Derrida emphasizes, is not itself bound by the rules of the structure—it is both outside the structure, in this sense, and inside the structure, since the center is a necessary part of the structure. This makes the center, in Derrida's words, "contradictorily coherent."

An example of a structure with a center might be a class in a school. The teacher creates the syllabus, determines where the students sit, what the students do, and how the students can interact within the structure. The teacher thus is the creator of the structure of the class, but s/he does not have to follow the rules s/he sets for the students: the teacher, for example, can talk without being called on. The teacher as center governs the classroom and is part of the classroom, but is also separate from it.

Derrida argues that all systems of Western philosophy have posited some sort of center, which guarantees the functioning and the truth of that system. The center of Christianity is the idea of God as the all-powerful Being who created the world, everything in it, and the rules that govern it, but who is not part of that world directly. Derrida reads the history of Western philosophy as the continual substitution of one center for another, without fundamentally changing the structure of elements organized by the center. Hence, human reason may be substituted as center in the place of God as Cartesian rationality replaces belief in a supreme being, and the Freudian unconscious replaces human reason as center as the belief in the powers of logic and reason to know the world completely gives way to Freud's idea that thoughts and desires we cannot know directly are the source of our actions and feelings.

The center is not named as "center" in these structures; rather, the center is an absolute or a priori truth, the axiom on which the rest of philosophy is built. Deconstruction is a process of finding and revealing the center of a system, showing how the center controls the relations of the elements. Deconstruction is the moment in which it is possible to see the center as a part of the structure, rather than simply as "truth," and to be aware of the "structurality of structure." Once the center, and its method for ordering the elements of the system, are revealed, deconstruction asks what might happen if the center were removed—how would the structure be altered? Would it fall apart?

Derrida reads Levi-Strauss as asserting that the fundamental structure of human thought is the binary opposition, and notes that the two sides of a binary opposition are held in place as opposites (good is what is not evil, evil is what is not good) by a center—in this example, God says what is good and what is evil, thus holding the binary opposition together. Deconstruction, in effect, wants to remove the center to study how the structure collapses or shifts.

The center keeps the elements from moving; this movement is what Derrida calls "play." The center limits play. Removing the center destabilizes the structure, and allows for more play among the elements. The bricoleur responds to this destabilization by putting together the elements of the decentered, deconstructed system in whatever way s/he wants, without regard to the previous system. The engineer responds by trying to rebuild the old system.

Colonialism

Colonialism is the act of becoming a colony. The era of colonialism began after the medieval period in Western Europe, when European explorers went around the world "discovering" new territories and claiming it for their own king or queen, as part of their own nation. Colonialism comes with the technological development of systems of navigation, the ability to chart the world, as well as from the development of better ships; the imperatives of trade, with burgeoning forms of capitalism, also demanded new sources of raw materials and new markets for manufactured goods. The emerging idea of a nation—a political entity defining membership in a specific social organization, under the control of a monarch or form of government—also encouraged exploration and colonization, as nations expanded their territories. The process of colonization included introducing Western European customs and culture to the indigenous population.

The idea of a colony was to form an outpost of one's own nation/culture in another land: to import that nation's customs, laws, educational and disciplinary systems, religions, and literature, and then to assert its culture as superior to the indigenous culture. Colonialism required both military force and ideological force; writings by the colonizers constructed the indigenous cultures as savage, primitive, and needing the guidance of the colonizers.

Condensation

Condensation is one of two main mechanisms that dreams use to disguise forbidden desires repressed within the unconscious. According to Freud, the unconscious contains all of the desires that are barred from our conscious awareness; the contents of the unconscious can only be accessed indirectly. Freud highlights three ways that the unconscious reveals these desires: through dreams, jokes, and slips of the tongue (parapraxes). Within each of these ways, repressed desires are coded into images, usually based on linguistic models or structures. The process of condensation allows a whole set of images or desires to be compressed into a single image. Condensation in psychoanalysis corresponds to metaphor in poetry, where one thing becomes another thing through a statement of identification: "love is a rose, and you'd better not pick it" says in essence that "love" and "rose" are the same thing.

Critical theory

Critical theory refers to the writings and philosophies emerging from the Frankfurt Institute of Social Research, established in 1923 in Frankfurt, Germany, to pursue studies in the humanities and social sciences that were independent of any public or private funding. "The Frankfurt School," as it became known, under the direction of Max Horkheimer, sponsored research in literary and aesthetic areas by thinkers such as Theodore Adorno, Leo Lowenthal, and Herbert Marcuse; the writings of Bertolt Brecht, Georg Lukacs, and Walter Benjamin were also associated with the Frankfurt School. Critical theory draws heavily on the works of Marx and Freud in investigating the operations of ideology; its goal was to find ways of understanding human culture that would help liberate people from the illusions of ideologies that distort or deny their objective interests. In this sense, Critical theory has more to do with Marxist sociological and political theory than with literary theory per se; its focus on ideology, however, led many members of the Frankfurt School to investigate the role literary texts play in creating and maintaining ideologies. Walter Benjamin, for example, argued that art and literature are not just reflections of social relations, but are among the many modes of production of social relations, as mediated by aesthetic (in contrast to economic) practices. The Frankfurt School closed in 1973 with the death of Max Horkheimer; Jürgen Habermas remains its most significant contemporary spokesperson.

Deconstruction

Deconstruction begins when Jacques Derrida observes, in "Structure, Sign and Play in the Discourse of the Human Sciences" (1966), that there is a "scandal" in Lévi-Strauss' analysis of the structure of myth and culture in *The Raw and the Cooked*. Lévi-Strauss argues that all mythology and indeed all human culture and human thought are structured by binary oppositions. Binary oppositions are by definition mutually exclusive; hot is what is not cold, night is what is not day, black is what is not white. Nothing on one side of the / (slash) can have anything in common with the thing on the other side of the /. Derrida looks at a particular binary opposition that Lévi-Strauss places at the center of his analysis: the opposition of nature/culture, which Lévi-Strauss aligns with a host of other binaries including raw/cooked, animal/human, and universal/specific. Within this binary opposition, however, Derrida finds something that belongs to both sides of the binary. He points out that the incest taboo—the prohibition in every human culture against having sexual relations with a blood relative—is universal therefore natural; every human culture has one. But the incest taboo differs in various cultures; in some cultures it is okay to have sexual relations with your first cousin, and in some cultures it is not. This means that the incest taboo is specific and cultural. That is the scandal! Derrida finds something that belongs to both sides of the /, something that is both nature and culture. His discovery is a challenge to the structural stability of the binary opposition; not only does it rattle the absolute distinction represented by the slash, but it rattles all other binary oppositions that depend on the slash making an unbreakable boundary between two sides defined as opposites.

Derrida then studies the consequences when other fundamental binary oppositions are destabilized. He focuses specifically on the binary opposition presence/absence, which is important in Plato's metaphysics; Plato associates presence or full presence with the ideal realm of the forms, and absence with material human existence here on earth. Presence is better than absence in Platonic philosophy, just as speech, because it represents presence, is better than writing, which represents absence. Speech is a guarantee of the presence of the person doing the speaking; writing marks the absence of the writer. Think about someone speaking in a classroom and writing on the board. For communication to happen between the speaker and the audience both have to be physically present at the moment of speaking; words written on the board, however, continue to have meaning even when the person who wrote these words is no longer in the classroom. In his book *Of Grammatology*, Derrida investigates the implications of destabilizing the binary pairs presence/absence and speech/writing, noting that Western philosophical traditions have followed Plato in valuing speech and presence—and all the other things to the left of the slash—over writing, absence, and the things to the right of the slash.

Derrida asserts that Western philosophy has privileged speech and presence over absence; perhaps the best example of that appears in the biblical account of creation. Creation begins when God speaks; the act of speaking guarantees that God exists, is present, and has the power to speak. God's speech—"let there be light"—creates light; God's speech has the power to make something out of nothing. Once God has made light by speaking, the binary opposite of light/dark exists, and it is God's will that holds the two binaries in opposition. The idea that words—"in the beginning was the word"—are a primary creative force is what Derrida calls logocentrism; logos meaning word or sometimes logic, and centrism meaning at the center. Western philosophy from Plato to Derrida has been logocentric, favoring speech over writing, presence over absence, light over dark, and all the binaries that become associated with these, including good/evil, male/female, white/black, reason/madness, order/chaos, and so on. Deconstruction for Derrida is a way of destabilizing these binary oppositions and seeing what happens to the certainty of our ideas and our philosophical systems when the binary structure on which they depend gets shaken up.

The fundamental method of deconstruction is to locate a binary opposition, find something that belongs to both sides of the slash, and begin to look for a logic or force that originally held the binary opposition in place. In the case of the binary opposition nature/

culture, Derrida finds the incest taboo belonging to both sides, which allows him to examine what makes nature and culture opposites—what kind of logic, what kind of thinking, what kind of worldview creates and depends upon nature and culture, each containing no element of the other.

In "Structure, Sign, and Play," Derrida argues that what holds binary oppositions in place has always been the notion of some sort of sense, that is, some power or force that creates a system of binary oppositions and keeps each piece of a binary on its proper side of the slash. An example of such a center might be God, as in my previous example. Derrida says that the history of Western philosophy reveals the continual substitution of one center for another, rather than any effort to form a structure not based on binary oppositions. If he were to write a history of Western philosophy, Derrida might say that it begins with Plato positing the ideal for the forms of the center, followed by Christianity positing God as the center, followed by the Enlightenment positing human reason or the I as the center (think of Descartes and "I think therefore I am"), followed by Freud positing the unconscious as the center of thought and action. The substitution of one center for another ended, according to Derrida, with his essay "Structure, Sign, and Play" in which he showed us how to see structures and their centers, and made it possible for us to think about "the structurality of structure."

When a center creates a system and holds all of the elements of the system in place—like keeping each side of the binary opposition on its proper side of the slash—the system is stable; its elements cannot move around much. When you remove the center of the system, nothing is holding the elements in place; the system is destabilized, and the elements have more "play." Play for Derrida is flexibility. In architecture or engineering, the word play refers to how much flexibility or movement a piece of material might have; in building a multi-storey office tower, architects and contractors want steel beams to have very little play, as the safety and stability of the building depend on the limitation of play or movement. Derrida chooses the word play in order to invoke its joyful childlike associations as well; play is fun. Removing the center from the system introduces play into the system by allowing the elements of the system more freedom of movement, and Derrida sees this as a positive thing. Play makes possible new combinations and arrangements of the elements of the system; when the center is removed, the elements do not have to follow the rules of the center, and thus can recombine in ways previously prevented by the center. You might think here about playing a game such as Monopoly or Parcheesi. The game contains playing pieces, a playing board, and rules for how to move the pieces around the board and how to win the game. At the center of the notion of the game is the idea that players follow the rules, that they play the game the way the people who made it intended it to be played. If you take out that center, you can play the game however you like; you can move around the board in the opposite direction or use the pieces for something completely different than as markers of the game or whatever you please. This is how kids play: if you introduce a bunch of kids to a room full of toys the kids will not play with the toys according to the rules of the toys. If there is a set of Legos, a set of dice, a deck of cards, and some modeling clay, the kids will mix up all the elements. They will play with things as they wish rather than according to any particular rules (i.e., if they are left to their own devices and not required to play in a particular way by a "center" such as an adult). The children in this example are performing what Derrida calls "bricolage," which is essentially making whatever you want with the elements at hand without regard for the original purpose of the elements or the original rules for putting those elements together. The engineer wants to see binary oppositions reestablished, probably starting with the binary opposition order/chaos; the bricoleur, the creative artist, has by contrast what poet John Keats called "negative capability," or the capacity to tolerate ambiguity, disorder, and uncertainty.

Desire

Desire is a complex term in literary and cultural theory, referring to specific concepts in psychoanalysis that have been adopted and modified by a number of post-structuralist theories. The term "desire" is most closely associated with Lacanian psychoanalysis; the French *désir* is Lacan's translation of Freud's German word *Wunsch*, also meaning wish. Desire for Lacan indicates an unfulfillable longing, which is necessarily a sexual or libidinal feeling. Desire is distinguished from need, which a child experiences as a biological imperative and which can be fulfilled, and from demand, in which a child gives verbal expression to needs; desire can never be satisfied by an object or a person. Rather, Lacan argues that desire is the result of the necessary splitting of the human mind into the ego and unconscious, into a notion of "self" and "other;" the fact of the split between the two (and the production of "self" from the notion of "otherness") can never be healed or reconciled. Thus desire is the human condition, the constant unattainable longing for a (re)union between self and other, or the deconstruction of the binary opposition conscious/unconscious and the complete dissolution of the ego.

Desire, for Lacan, is always founded on lack or absence. Desire is the awareness of the fact of lack, that absence exists, rather than the search for something to fill any particular lack. The idea of human existence as founded on lack comes from Plato, who sees human love and sexuality as the neverending search for completion, unity, or wholeness; this idea reappears frequently in Western philosophy from Descartes to Hegel.

Diachronic

Diachronic refers to any kind of analysis or investigation of how events change over time. The study of history for example is often diachronic, trying to account for how things change over time. This term stands in binary opposition to synchronic, meaning any kind of analysis that does not take time into account. Structuralism usually relies on synchronic analysis; that is, it looks at a structure at a particular moment in time as if that structure had always existed and would always exist exactly the way it is at the moment of observation. Synchronic analyses are not interested in change or development, nor in origin or endpoint; a synchronic analysis looks at something at a single moment in time. Diachronic analysis, in contrast, looks specifically for origins and changes as it examines a structure or phenomenon over a period of time. Structuralist analysis in linguistics, anthropology, and sociology are primarily synchronic forms of analysis; a structuralist analysis of the signifying system would be interested only in investigating what the structure is at a particular moment and not in determining how the system has changed or how it began.

Dialogic

Dialogic is a term associated primarily with the works of Mikhail Bakhtin, a literary and linguistic theorist working in the Soviet Union in the 1920s, whose works were not discovered by Western thinkers until the 1960s. Bakhtin was not a Marxist or a post-structuralist, but rather a thinker interested in the social relations inherent in any form of speech or writing. He contrasts the unitary, single-voiced speech of the monologue, where only one person is speaking, with the idea of dialogue, where two or more voices engage with each other from different points of view. Monologue, or monologia, is associated with the idea of a centralized power system, a single voice speaking the only truth that can exist, without challenge or interplay. Dialogic speech, on the other hand, always involves a multiplicity of speakers and a variety of perspectives; truth becomes something negotiated and debated, rather than something pronounced from on high. Monologic speech seems to come from God or nowhere; it is dissociated from the speaker who originates it, and from the social relations in which that speaker is embedded. Dialogic speech acknowledges sets of social relations between and among speakers, and is thus more descriptive of historical and cultural realities.

Bakhtin uses the concept of dialogism in discussing the distinction between novels and poetry as literary forms. In poetry, Bakhtin argues, words are used monologically, as if they have no connection to social or historical relations; a word has meaning only in reference to language itself. In prose fiction, by contrast, words are used dialogically, as having both etymological meaning and social meaning. The form of the novel, as exemplified in Dostoevsky, encourages dialogic speech, as different characters speak in recognizably different voices, and engage with each other in debating worldviews, rather than affirming a single worldview.

Another aspect of Bakhtin's dialogics appears in his discussions of the "double-voiced" word, a term he uses to describe irony or parody, or words used in quotation marks. A double-voiced word contains two meanings: a literal or monologic meaning, that is, a dictionary definition, and an implied or dialogic meaning, which appears in the social relationship between the two participants in a dialogue. An example is the word "smart." A monologic utterance would come from an authority, like a professor, who would describe a student by saying "she is very smart," which the listener would take at face value. Said between two students who dislike this person, however, "she is very smart" takes on another tone, one of irony or disbelief—an added "yeah, right" that designates a worldview shared by the two speakers, but not by the person referred to. This double-voiced word is similar to the concept of the double-voiced discourse articulated by W. E. B. du Bois in discussing the experience of African Americans who learn to speak two languages: that of the dominant white culture and that of their black subculture.

Différance

Différance is the term coined by Jacques Derrida to express how meaning in language is always provisional rather than definite. *Différance* comes from the French verb "*différer*," which means both "to differ" and "to defer." The distinction between the French "*différence*" and "*différance*" is visible in writing but not audible in speech; this is Derrida's deliberate attempt to emphasize the primacy of writing over speech, thus reversing the usual Western philosophical order. The idea of "*différance*" as "differing" comes from Saussure's concept of value, where meaning results from each element in a signifying system being different from all the other elements; thus you cannot know the meaning of a single element unless and until you know all the elements in the system. The idea of "*différance*" as "deferral" emphasizes that stable, final, or definitive meaning is impossible within such a system, as ultimate meaning is always "deferred" onto another element of the system. Différance, according to Derrida, is the constant shifting and sliding of one sign onto the next, and thus the constant slipperiness of any definitive meaning; this sliding can be stopped, or stabilized, when a center regulates the movement of the elements of the system, as the Phallus does for Lacan's idea of the Symbolic Order.

Discourse

Discourse is a term associated primarily with Michel Foucault's archaeological and genealogical investigations into the creation of the human sciences. In his early works, he discusses discursive formations as bodies of writing that constituted knowledge of a particular subject or idea; discourse here is equivalent to archive, or to written records. In his later genealogical works, Foucault examines both discursive and non-discursive practices and how both produce networks of power/knowledge.

The dictionary defines "discourse" as spoken or written expression; it tends to imply a formal argument, like an essay, as in Descartes' *Discourse on Method*. Foucault uses discourse to refer to a body of writings that form what can be said or known about a particular topic; the discourse on a topic limits and defines how a topic can be conceptualized and acted upon. An example is soccer. Think of everything that has ever been written on soccer: rules, history, biographies of players, news stories of games, sociological studies of soccer crowds, medical studies of soccer injuries, laws about soccer as a public event, the impact of television on the global popularity of soccer, the relation between soccer competition and national identity—the list could go on forever. All of these writings put together constitute the discourse on soccer; everything that can be said or known about soccer, in any aspect, is contained within this discourse. The discourse on soccer exists not just as an archive, however, but as the episteme within which soccer is enacted; how the game is played, understood, argued about, loved, and hated are all created by the terms of the discourse on soccer.

Displacement

Displacement is one of the primary mechanisms that dreams use to disguise forbidden desires repressed within the unconscious. The process of displacement starts with a desire that the unconscious mind cannot allow the conscious mind to know; the unconscious then produces an image of something close to or related to the forbidden desire, and allows that image to slip into the conscious mind in the form of a dream or a joke. Displacement allows a repressed desire to take on an image that can be consciously known. Displacement in psychoanalysis corresponds to metonymy in poetry, where one thing is replaced by something associated with it or representing it. A common definition of metonymy is referring to a part of something instead of naming the whole thing: for example, saying "the crown" when you mean the king, queen, or royalty.

Engineer

The engineer is the opposite of the bricoleur, the person who employs bricolage as a means to put together seemingly incompatible elements of a deconstructed system. The engineer, according to Derrida, wants to build things (buildings or philosophical systems) that are ordered and coherent, follow a plan, and use specific materials designed for the project at hand. The engineer dislikes "play," or the free movement of elements without a governing principle or center, and tries to build things that are stable, unmoving, solid, and thus "true."

English

English is a language, an ethnicity, and a scholarly discipline. What's the connection? The language evolved with the conquest of Scotland, Wales, and Ireland and the creation of the nation of Great Britain, whose official language is English. English is the hallmark of English colonies—the language of the colonizer replaced whatever language people spoke before colonization.

Literary studies called "English" are part of this. Literary studies started as a means of canonizing English literature by writing about it, studying it, teaching it, and printing it. English literature spread to all the places that Great Britain went; in British colonies, indigenous people learned to speak English and learned to read and value English literature as being better than their existing literary traditions. "English" today denotes both the study of literature in English and the study of the language itself, including debates about proper or correct meaning and grammar.

Episteme

Episteme is the Greek word for "knowledge"; Michel Foucault uses it to describe the overarching idea or conceptualization that links various writings to make a discourse or discursive formation. The episteme is not a type of knowledge, but rather the precondition for knowledge in any particular era, the framework or box within which scholars and writers think, but which is usually invisible to them as a framework. In *The Order of Things*, Foucault discusses two shifts in the episteme, from the Renaissance to the Classical age (the Enlightenment), and from the Classical age to the modern era (beginning of the nineteenth century). These shifts were not evolutionary or developmental, but discontinuous—each was a new worldview or way to think about thinking. In the Renaissance, for example, the episteme was based on the concept of resemblance—you could know what something was because you could find a resemblance between that thing and something else. All Renaissance cultural work, including philosophy, science, and literature, utilized this episteme.

Essentialism

Essentialism is a concept central to humanism; it is the idea that everything has a core essence that is unchanging and that constitutes the foundation of its being. The idea is articulated by Aristotle in his *Metaphysics*, where he asserts that the primary function of human reason is to discover the essence of phenomena. Essentialism in twentieth-century Western thought is associated with identity, with the idea that the human self has some universal and unalterable characteristics, including gender, race, sex, and sexuality. Essentialism is the viewpoint that you are born with certain innate traits that cannot be changed or altered by anything external. In the case of sex and gender, essentialists argue that one is male or female, and thus masculine or feminine, and that these categories exist eternally and universally. Essentialism is critiqued by most post-structuralist theories, which argue that all forms of human identity and being are socially and culturally constructed, and are therefore mutable.

Ethnicity

Ethnicity means specific to a particular culture. Everyone has an ethnicity—at least one—whether you identify it as "ethnic" or not. It is not the same as race—it is the people you grow up with, the world you first inhabit, your mother tongue, your father's folkways, what you learn you are like—what you identify with as a kid, as a family member, as a member of some kind of cultural group. We think of ethnicity in terms of the markers of culture: ethnic foods, ethnic crafts, ethnic speech, ethnic beliefs. That point of view is usually from those who do not consider themselves ethnic—for example, white ethnicity often is invisible, taken as the norm or the standard rather than as something "different." The hegemony of whiteness in the United States has given the word ethnic the status of "otherness"; "ethnic studies," for example, are assumed to include Hispanic, black, native American, and Asian cultures, but not white culture.

Father

In Freudian psychoanalysis, the term father refers to the male parent involved in a child's life. For Freud, the father was part of a nuclear family arrangement, consisting of mother, father, and child, wherein the father did not directly nurture the child but rather was the source of authority in the household. While the Freudian mother is posited as the primary source of the child's pleasure and hence the first object of its libidinal energy, the Freudian father breaks up the union between mother and child, claiming the mother as his own source of (specifically sexual) pleasure. The rivalry that develops between the child and the father for possession of the mother is enacted in the Oedipus Complex, wherein a boy wishes to kill the father and have the mother, as source of pleasure, all to himself. This OEDIPUS COMPLEX is resolved by the fear of castration, which Freud describes specifically as the (boy) child's fantasy that the father will cut off his penis if he continues to harbor the wish to kill his father and to feel a sexual/pleasurable connection (which Freud calls "libidinal cathexis") toward his mother. The father's authority and power are then internalized (by the boy) in the creation of the conscience or superego, while the desire for the mother is repressed, thus creating the unconscious.

   For Jacques Lacan, Father refers to a structural position rather than to a specific person. The Father, or The Name of the Father, or The Law of the Father is how Lacan refers to the position that serves as a center in the SYMBOLIC ORDER. He identifies this position with the Freudian father also by calling it the Phallus, emphasizing that it is through the father's threat to castrate the (boy) child that the latter must finally acknowledge the concept of lack or absence. For Lacan, the child's entry into the Symbolic Order, which means taking up a position within the structure of language so that signifiers (like "I" and "you") have specific meaning, happens when the child accepts the necessity of lack or absence, and the fact or concept of "otherness." This acceptance creates the ego within a field of desire, where the self ("I") is defined by lack, and the idea of fullness or presence (not lacking) is represented in the position of the center—or Phallus, or Father.

Feminist theory

Gender is a cultural universal; human bodies have two general forms that we label as male and female, and which all cultures associate with specific notions of what is masculine and what is feminine. Throughout human history cultures have operated on the basis of gender being a binary system, today, however, we are aware that human bodies can have a variety of sexual markers, making the division of each individual into a category that is either male or female highly problematic. Like all binaries, one term is what it is because it is not its opposite; male is what is not female, and female is what is not male, feminine is what is not masculine, and masculine is what is not feminine.

For as long as this binary structure for assigning social meaning to biologically dimorphic bodies has existed, there have been people who questioned and criticized how their culture constructed gender roles, particularly in cultures where what is gendered female or feminine is valued less or subordinated to what is male or masculine. In Western culture, feminists since the Middle Ages have been asking whether gender is biological, God-given, or otherwise immutable, universal, and unchangeable, or whether gender is a social construct, and therefore changeable. A common definition of 'feminist' is someone who sees an inequality between male and female forms of power and privilege, with women being subordinated to men, and who wants to change that system.

The theory part of feminist theory is simply the way that any feminist individual or feminist movement understands how gender inequality is created and perpetuated, and the ideas they have about how to change the status quo. There are as many different kinds of feminist theory as there are ways of understanding how gender differentiations are created.

In literary theory, feminist theory usually refers to two strains of thought concerning the relations between gender and writing. The first strain is Anglo-American, emerging in the late 1960s and 1970s in correlation with what is called the "women's liberation movement." This strain of feminist literary theory argued that literary studies have always been male dominated, and that our notions of what constitutes good or great literature have always been shaped by male models and male authors. This line of feminist literary theory, best exemplified by Sandra Gilbert and Susan Gubar in their work *The Madwoman in the Attic* (1980), searches for the works of forgotten female authors and calls for the reevaluation of writing by women through the development of a female-based or non-gendered standard of literary criticism.

The second strain comes from what has been called "French feminism," as named in the title of the first English language anthology of writings called *New French Feminisms* (1980); a more accurate name might be post-structural feminist theory. Rather than examining women and men and the power inequalities between them, post-structural feminist theory investigates "man" and "woman" as subject positions within the structure of language. Such theory sees male and female, masculine and feminine, as part of the Western logocentric structure of binary oppositions, and works to deconstruct these binaries; it examines how, and with what consequences, "woman" and "the feminine" are constructed as "otherness," as non-being, as something outside of and threatening to the consciousness, rationality, and presence valued in Western humanist thought. Post-structural feminist theorists include Hélène Cixous, Luce Irigaray, and Julia Kristeva.

Formalism

Formalism is a mode of literary analysis that focuses primarily on the literary text itself, without regard to the context of its creation or consumption. Formalism emerged in the 1920s as a way to separate literary studies from other disciplines such as history, sociology, and psychology; formalism was designed to define literary studies as its own form of knowledge, with its own unique object and methods of study. Formalists focus solely on what they call "literary facts," meaning the language of the literary text, arguing that literary language calls attention to its own status as language, rather than to the objects or concepts the words represent. In most formalist studies, "literature" is synonymous with "poetry," which has led to the criticism that formalism neglects drama, fiction, and other non-poetic literary forms. A movement known as Russian formalism developed in Moscow in the 1920s, led by Roman Jakobson, who viewed poetics as a subset of linguistics, and differentiated between the practical language of everyday life and the poetic language that characterized literary works. Russian formalism was attacked by the Soviets under Trotsky, who supported the Marxist idea that literary studies should always describe the relations between a literary text and the social and economic factors that determined its production. Because of this, Russian formalism was suppressed, and none of its critical writings appeared in the West until the 1950s and 1960s, when it informed the structuralism of Roland Barthes and Gerard Genette. Though the Anglo-American "New Criticism" was also a formalist method, it was not influenced by Russian formalism.

Fort/Da

This phrase refers to a particular anecdote in Freud's work *Beyond the Pleasure Principle* (1920). Freud observes his nephew, aged about 18 months, playing a game wherein he throws a spool of thread away from him and says *Fort*, the German word for "gone," and then reels the spool back in, saying *Da*, the German word for "here." In this fort/da game, Freud sees the child trying to cope with his sense of anxiety around absence (for Freud, the absence or loss of the mother) by replaying the moment of separation ("gone") and then experiencing the pleasure of the return of the lost object ("here"). Freud reads this as the child's effort to gain mastery over anxiety by repeating the process of trauma and recovery.

Lacan takes this anecdote and focuses on the elements of language at work within it. He says the boy, at 18 months, is just beginning his entry into the Symbolic Order, into the structure of language. The boy is enacting the experience of loss, which Lacan says is the basis for language: entry into the Symbolic Order requires that the child separate itself from its mother and accept the concepts of "otherness" and "lack." Lacan argues that the boy's articulation of lack, in saying the word *fort*, highlights his position as a speaking, language-using subject, who now has a "self" that uses words as a kind of compensation for accepting "otherness" as the condition of existence of the self.

Gay

Gay is a term popularly associated with homosexuality, usually referring to male homosexuals rather than lesbians, but is used as a collective adjective (and sometimes noun) for both sexes. The origins of the term date back to the nineteenth-century Western sexual underworld, where "gay" was a code word for "prostitute" or other illicit forms of sex. It began to take on its contemporary meaning in the 1920s, and gained widespread usage in the 1960s, with the emergence of the Gay Liberation Front and Gay Pride movements in the United States and Europe. The greater visibility of male homosexuals in these movements led to the word "gay" implying men, so that frequently organizations add other letters to their names to include lesbians, bisexuals, and transgendered people (GLBT).

The gaze

The gaze is the English translation of the French phrase "le regard," used by Sartre and Lacan to refer to the mechanism by which a self is regarded or seen by others. Lacan emphasizes the importance of visual perception in the process of the mirror phase, when a child sees its reflection in a mirror and gives that reflection the label "self" or "me." The mirror phase constitutes a misrecognition only possible through the register of the visible, as the child sees itself for the first time in the image in the mirror, which it perceives as an integrated whole. Prior to this moment, the child's perception of its own body was fragmented; it had never seen its body as a whole. With the visual perception of its mirror image, the child misidentifies its self with the visual image of a whole person, in relation to which image the self will always be lacking or will fall short. The self, for Lacan, is constituted by the gaze, by the visual act of seeing an other and internalizing that as "self."

The gaze also has power in Lacanian psychoanalysis because of its ability to detect presence and absence. This comes from Freud's insistence that the penis is the superior organ because it is visible; female genitalia are "nothing" for Freud because they are not unitary and visible like the penis. Lacan translates this into the idea of the Phallus (or Other or Name of the Father) as the marker of full presence, the place where there is no lack or absence. As the mode by which male spectators perceive the "nothingness" of femaleness, the gaze is phallocentric, and functions to objectify women and to render them as objects rather than as subjects or selves.

Gender

Gender is a cultural universal; all cultures have some means of distinguishing between male and female, masculine and feminine. Gender often seems to be the natural or innate expression of biological sex: a female is gendered feminine, a male gendered masculine. However, neither sex nor gender operates quite as simply as that. Biological sex is determined (or overdetermined) by multiple factors, including external genitalia (penis or clitoris/vagina), internal reproductive organs (ovaries, uterus, testes), chromosomal sex (XX or XY), and secondary sex characteristics (body hair, breasts). Thus the division of all humans into the binary categories of male or female appears in contemporary biology as an oversimplification. So too does the relationship between sex and gender: biological sex does not determine gender expression. From a post-structuralist perspective, gender consists of sets of cultural signifiers that are associated with the signified of a particular sexed body. Every culture that recognizes sexual dimorphism (male and female) also creates cultural categories of masculine and feminine. Lipstick and high heels, in Western culture, are signifiers that presumably point to a female body, while a moustache and a hard hat presumably point to a male body. These signifiers, however, are not fixed and stable, but mutable and arbitrary—what constitutes "feminine" and "masculine" changes through historical shifts and cultural movements. The color pink, now firmly associated with girl babies, used to be thought of as a strong, masculine color, while blue was the gentler, more feminine color. The mutability of gender allows for much play, as in cross-dressing; one's gender expression can vary from moment to moment, and from situation to situation, rather than being a necessarily stable and essential aspect of one's identity.

Genealogy of knowledge

Genealogy of knowledge is the phrase used to describe the methodologies of Michel Foucault's works in the latter period of his life. A genealogist is someone who looks at families and descendents, at how people are variously related to their forbears and to each other. Foucault's genealogy examines how specific institutions and social practices interact to create forms of knowledge and technologies of power in which the human subject is enmeshed. To his archaeological work with archives, Foucault adds concern with non-discursive practices and an interrogation of how power and knowledge work together to create our ideas and practices about "the human" within the human sciences; he is particularly interested, in his genealogical work, on how forms of power/knowledge produce and regulate notions about the human body. Works considered "genealogical" include *Discipline and Punish* and *The History of Sexuality* (Vols. 1–3).

Grammatology

Grammatology is the study of writing or the history of alphabets and modes of scribing. The term is usually associated with Jacques Derrida's book *Of Grammatology* (1967), which offered a critical examination of the Western philosophical traditions of phonocentrism—favoring speech over writing, the audible word over the written word—and logocentrism.

Grand narrative

This is a term associated most often with François Lyotard and his theories about postmodernism. A grand narrative, or metanarrative, is literally a big story; a story that gives other stories credence or truth value. The "grand narrative" of Marxism, for instance, is that capitalism will ultimately be destroyed in favor of socialist utopian communities; this will mark the end of class struggle and thus the end of history. The "grand narrative" of democracy, in contrast, is that democracy, or one person–one vote, is the best, most egalitarian form of government, and that universal democracy will guarantee individual rights and freedom. Such grand narratives, according to Lyotard, function as "truth"; a grand narrative then serves as validation and proof of all the narratives that it can contain and encompass, and likewise also serves as disproof and invalidation of all the narratives that it cannot contain, which are then by definition "false." Grand narratives are part of modernity; the modern world depends upon such "big stories" to legitimate practices (such as the invasion of a country in order to force it to become democratic), which otherwise would expose contradictions and conflicts. The postmodern perspective on grand narratives, for Lyotard, is one of skepticism and deconstruction; no one single narrative speaks truth, or has any more power or explanatory value than any other. Legitimation, or the establishment of something as "true," comes from local or micronarratives, stories told about what happens in a particular place at a particular time, without reference to some larger context or framework. An election in Afghanistan, then, would be the story of an election, not of the larger march of progress toward worldwide democracy.

Hegemony

Hegemony describes the kind of cultural power wielded by the dominant ideas of a culture or society; it derives from the Greek *hegemon*, meaning leader or dominant force. The term is associated primarily with Antonio Gramsci, who discusses how ideologies are produced and disseminated within a capitalist culture. Gramsci makes a distinction between ideologies produced and enforced by the state, which are directly shaped by the interests of the ruling classes, and ideologies produced through civil society, through forms of representation that are not directly and overtly connected to state control. The ideologies produced and circulated within civil society create a worldview that becomes popular and pervasive; rather than being identified with the ruling class, these ideologies establish hegemony in being adopted and enacted by most of the population. An idea or belief becomes hegemonic when it becomes the dominant idea in civil society; hegemony is created and maintained at different levels by academic intellectuals, and by the educational system, mass media, and cultural institutions such as religions and politics. Hegemony is established when a particular belief or worldview becomes ubiquitous—when a particular way of seeing and explaining the world appropriates all rival or oppositional modes of thinking. An idea is hegemonic when you cannot think outside of its box, when it seems to all—ruling classes and civil society—to describe the truth.

Hermeneutics

Hermeneutics is a Greek word meaning to translate, to make clear and understandable; it is associated with the Greek god Hermes, who interpreted the cryptic messages of the gods for mortals. Hermeneutics in literary theory can be defined as the theory of the science or methods of interpretation employed in reading literary and cultural texts. What we call hermeneutics began as scriptural exegesis; during the Protestant Reformation, the question of whether priests or laypeople had the authority to interpret the Bible brought hermeneutics to the forefront of religious reform. By the nineteenth century in Europe hermeneutics had become the methodology of textual interpretation—theories of how one read and made sense of cultural symbols or texts, including literary texts, not limited to scripture. Friedrich Schleiermacher articulated the fundamental premise of hermeneutics as the "hermeneutic circle," wherein a part of something is always understood in terms of the whole, and vice-versa. An example of this would be a sentence: you know the meaning of a sentence by knowing the meaning of the individual words in the sentence, and you know the meaning of the individual words by understanding the sentence as a whole. In the twentieth century, hermeneutics became allied with structuralist and post-structuralist thought, and with reader-response theory; its philosophy was that to understand human beings is to understand human cultural expression, in whatever form. Theorists associated with hermeneutics include Wilhelm Dilthey, Hans-Georg Gadamer, Martin Heidegger, and Paul Ricoeur.

Heteroglossia

Heteroglossia a term associated with Mikhail Bakhtin's theories of the novel. Heteroglossia means literally a variety of languages; for Bakhtin, heteroglossia is the variety of discourses, or kinds of socially constructed speech, that are employed in any dialogic interaction. An example of heteroglossia is the different kinds of language one employs in the course of the day: you speak differently to your professor than you do to your friends or to your parents or to a police officer. The kind of language you use is created by your social relationship to the person you are talking to; to a professor or police officer, you are more likely to speak formally, politely, and deferentially than you would to a friend or family member. Each social interaction determines what kind of social speech (sociolect) you choose to use; each sociolect speaks from a worldview shared by the two speakers involved in the dialogue. Heteroglossia is thus the sum of all the sociolects employed by any speaker in any situation.

Bakhtin argues that the form of the novel is inherently heteroglossic; novels employ different voices through different characters, and use different discourses to create a variety of worldviews. Novels told from a single perspective or authorial stance tend to be monologic; novels narrated from multiple perspectives employ heteroglossia to create multiple viewpoints and explanations. An example of a heteroglossic novel is Melville's *Moby Dick*, which uses a vast variety of discourses to explain the world. Melville includes the language of Calvinist Christianity, which describes a world dominated by sin and predestination; he also includes the language of capitalism, which describes a world more concerned with profit and loss than with salvation. Each language or discourse Melville uses—from the natural history of whales to the mythology of the American frontier—creates a different way of understanding the world that his words and characters create.

Humanism

Humanism is one of those gigantic "umbrella" terms that can mean just about anything. In literary studies, humanism basically refers to a philosophical perspective that places the human, rather than the divine or the natural, at the center of investigation: humanists are interested in what humans do, think, say, make, and believe, rather than in what God does or what Nature does. Humanism is often called "liberal humanism," with the connotation that a human-centered worldview must be inclusive and accepting of all the ways of being human; in this sense humanism is contrasted to religious doctrines, which dictate particular modes of action and thought. Humanism is also associated with the humanities, the branches of study that investigate what and how humans create, think about, and organize their worlds; the departments of English, history, languages, philosophy, and art constitute "the humanities" within a university system.

Humanism in Western thought refers roughly to a shared set of ideas and values about being human. These include the following:

1. That there exists in each human an entity we call the "self," which is a unique form of being. This self is capable of rational thought and of self-representation in language (via the word "I"). While each person has a unique individual self, each self also has universal characteristics shared with all other selves. This self is essential—it never changes, regardless of external circumstances.

2. That there is a real world external to the self, which the self can perceive, observe, and reason about. This process of observation and reason to explain the external world is called "science"; science is objective and produces universal truth.

3. That language exists to represent the external world and to express the interior workings of the self. Individuals use language to create new ways to express their own unique experiences of being human.

Humanist thought faced a number of challenges in the twentieth century, particularly from Marxism and psychoanalysis; during the political upheavals in the Western world in the 1960s and 1970s, humanism was discredited by the premises of post-structuralist theory.

Hybrid

In the biological sciences, a hybrid is a combination or mixture of two distinct genetic lines that create an entirely new variety or type; most agricultural practices, both ancient and modern, rely on crossing different varieties of plants and animals to create hybrid offspring. In the postmodern sense, a hybrid is any phenomenon that mixes elements from two distinct traditions or practices. Most post-structuralist theory, for instance, is a hybrid of various modes of thought or disciplines: psychoanalytic, Marxist, linguistic, anthropological, literary. Hybridity often causes deconstruction, as a hybrid necessarily belongs to at least two categories at once; within a system of binary oppositions, a hybrid belongs to both sides, and thus destabilizes the idea of "opposition" itself.

Hybridity often comes up in postcolonial theory as a way to describe emerging forms of identity and status that arise in the postcolonial and postmodern world. Homi Bhaba discusses hybridity as the place between two conflicting cultures or moments, when identities are destabilized and deconstructed. One is a hybrid if one belongs to more than one identity category, such as being Islamic (religious) and Turkish (national). Identity categories based on race, class, gender, and nationality, Bhaba argues, are continually being challenged and undermined by hybridity, by people who move across boundaries and inhabit the "in-between" spaces of cultures. The backlash to postmodern hybridity is the attempt to "purify" a race, culture, or ethnicity, often by genocide; "ethnic cleansing" to eliminate people who do not fit within single identity categories is an attempt to exterminate hybridity.

Hyperreality

Hyperreality is a reality that is too real to be real. It is a combination of the idea of "reality" with the Greek word *hyper*, meaning "over" or "beyond." The term was used first by Umberto Eco to describe museums and amusement parks in the United States that try to produce a reality based on illusion and representation. An example is a commercial for a television set: the TV set is shown at the edge of the Grand Canyon; on the TV screen is a picture of the Grand Canyon, and the people in the commercial are watching the TV image rather than the actual Grand Canyon in front of them. The TV picture is hyperreal—more real to the viewers in the commercial than the actual phenomenon. Postmodern theorists like Eco and Baudrillard argue that American culture in particular is obsessed with the hyperreal; parks like Disneyland (now also popular in Europe) create a version of "reality" that is more stable, predictable, and satisfying than actual reality. Hyperreality creates events and environments that are so "life-like" the observer cannot tell the difference between the creation and the actual world; postmodern theorists argue that such hyperreality replaces and erases the actual, so that only the hyperreal world exists.

Hypertext

In information technology, hypertext is made by following hyperlinks on the internet. What we now refer to simply as "links," the underlined or highlighted words or phrases on a web page that take you to another web page, were originally called "hyperlinks" to denote that they link two virtual electronic sites, rather than connecting two physical sites (as the links in a chain do). In the early days of the internet, a hypertext was created by combining hyperlinks to create a "text" made of images, sounds, words, and other electronically transmissible media; today we might call a hypertext simply a web page.

In the 1990s, many writers experimented with how the new medium of computers and information technology could transform literary genres. The "hypernovel" consisted of a story told with embedded hyperlinks, so that the reader could click on any hyperlink and take a different path in the story being told. Such hypertexts transformed the idea of linear narrative and authorial control, as readers could construct their own version of a story depending on what links they chose to follow.

The term hypertext predates computers, however; Gerard Genette used "hypertext" to refer to any literary work that was made up of, or made reference to, any previous literary work; he called such works "second-degree" literature. Examples of Genette's hypertexts include James Joyce's *Ulysses,* as well as a number of Western texts that refer to previous texts (such as Fielding's *Shamela,* a parodic rewrite of Richardson's *Pamela*).

Hysteria

Hysteria comes from the Greek word *hystera*, meaning "uterus." The Greeks believed the uterus had a life or will of its own, and a woman who did not bear children risked having her uterus wander about her body causing disorder and illness. In its modern sense, hysteria denotes an overwrought and excessive emotional reaction to an event or circumstance; because of its Greek roots, the idea of hysteria has long been associated with women and femininity. Sigmund Freud investigated hysteria to try to explain why a body might have physical symptoms (such as paralysis) that were not caused by any empirical organic condition. In his examinations of women patients suffering from hysteria, he came to the conclusion that hysteria was a form of neurosis, a means by which repressed unconscious desires could be articulated in the form of symptoms. His insistence that hysteria was a psychological, rather than a physiological, problem led to the development of the "talking cure," another name for psychoanalysis. Feminist theorists such as Hélène Cixous have re-examined Freud's descriptions of hysterical women, arguing that hysteria is a reaction to patriarchal oppression, and a means for women who are barred from full access to representational language in the Lacanian Symbolic realm to speak through their bodies in a mode disruptive to the phallogocentric order.

Id

Id is a translation of the German phrase "das Es," or "the it." Id is the name given by Sigmund Freud to the unconscious. The id is one of the three areas of the mind or psyche; the others are the ego or self, and the superego or conscience. The id is where original sexual desires, which Freud names libidinal drives, are repressed through the process of sublimation, and the subordination of the Pleasure Principle to the Reality Principle. The self or ego, the entity that says "I," is barred from the id, or "it," which exists as the I's "other"; but the boundary between ego and id is permeable, with elements of id always on the edges of the ego/consciousness.

Lacan translates "das Es" into the French phrase "le ça," or "the it." The unconscious, for Lacan, is constituted by signifiers, rather than by biological drives or desires; he asserts that "the unconscious is structured like a language," describing id as endless intersecting chains of signifiers in constant circulation, where there exist no signifieds to create a stable sign or definitive meaning. The ego or self is produced when the child enters into the Symbolic realm; the ego is subordinated to the rules of language, in obedience to the stabilization of the Phallus as center, and exists then as a subject within language, subject to the rules of language.

Ideology

Ideology is, literally, the study or science of ideas. The term has a wide range of meanings in various theories, but generally means the systems of beliefs and ideas available within any particular culture. Examples of ideologies within any culture may include religious beliefs, political beliefs, and aesthetic ideals. Classical Marxism saw ideology as part of the superstructure, the cultural practices and ideas that were shaped by the economic base; ideology in this sense constituted the ideas of the ruling class, and was the equivalent of "false consciousness," a kind of illusion that kept people from grasping the scientific or objective truth about their real conditions of existence. Later Marxists, including Antonio Gramsci, argued that ideology was relatively autonomous from the economic base, that there was no simple cause and effect relationship between the modes and forces of production in any society and the way members of that society thought and acted. Louis Althusser's explanation of ideology insisted that a person's ideological beliefs always appeared in material form through that person's actions and choices; you show what you believe when you behave in a certain way. Althusser showed how ideology interpellates or calls to individuals, persuading them to inhabit a particular worldview or subject position within which a specific ideology seems merely "true." Althusser also distinguished between ideologies, which have specific content, and Ideology as a structural component of social organization. Ideology, he argues, is ahistorical—all cultures have some kind of ideology, some structure for the dissemination and production of ideas and beliefs. Ideologies, however, are historically specific, and can be changed and altered by social movements. In this sense, for Althusser, Ideology is the form that beliefs take, and ideologies are the specific content of Ideology. Marxists tend to privilege science as an objective mode of knowing that transcends ideologies and professes truth; this analysis fails to consider science itself as an ideology.

Imaginary

The Imaginary is one of three realms described by Jacques Lacan that a child must pass through to become a linguistic speaking subject. The first of these realms, the Real, is marked by the child's non-differentiation from anything or anyone around it; in the Real, there are no images, no representations, and no language because the child does not know any separation between self and other. The child must leave the Real due to the imperatives of biological growth, as it begins to recognize its body as being distinct from that of its mother or caregivers. When the child begins to use images for its psychological development—such as internalizing an image of a face—it enters the Imaginary realm. Within the Imaginary, the child experiences the mirror phase, in which it sees its own reflection in a mirror and misrecognizes that specular or visual experience as a representation of itself. The child thus internalizes an Imaginary specular image of a whole body, which comes to replace its fragmentary experience of its own body parts. Lacan argues that the visual or specular self internalized in the Imaginary becomes the basis for the linguistic speaking self—the self who says "I"—in the Symbolic Order. There is no clear division between the Imaginary and the Symbolic, and humans as subjects are always misrecognizing images as a form of reality. The Imaginary is thus associated with creativity, with poetry, and with the powers of the imagination.

Interpellation

Interpellation is a term used by Louis Althusser in his discussion of how Ideology and ideologies operate within a culture. The word comes from the term "appellation," meaning a name; to interpellate is to call someone by name, to recognize them. Althusser insists that ideologies exist only by and for subjects—someone has to believe in an idea, and practice that belief, for an ideology to exist. Ideologies thus must always be recruiting subjects, getting people to believe in them as "truth," and to act accordingly. This recruiting is what Althusser calls "interpellation." An ideology or belief system calls to a subject—it says, "Hey, you!" and the subject responds—in an act of mutual recognition: the ideology names the subject, and the subject confirms his or her recognition of the ideology. An example might be religious conversion, where a person hears a particular theology being explained, and feels that the message is being addressed to him or her personally. This kind of interpellation occurs constantly in media images, particularly in advertising, when a commercial asks if "you" want to have a certain kind of product; those who hear "you" as naming them specifically—"who, me?"—are interpellated into the belief system created by the advertisement: "why yes, I do want to have a healthier body" (e.g.). Cultural texts, including literary texts, work to interpellate consumers to create the effect of realism; a successfully interpellated moviegoer will inhabit the viewer position created by the film, and will thus enter into the story and worldview of the movie. The direct address of the consumer is a mode of interpellation; when a literary text says "Oh, dear reader, haven't you ever felt this way?" the text is working to position the reader within its particular ideology. The experience of not being able to "get into" a text is often the result of an unsuccessful interpellation.

Intertextuality

Intertextuality means the interaction of texts. Coined by Julia Kristeva in reference to Mikhail Bakhtin's ideas of heteroglossia, intertextuality posits that a text (literary or non-literary) never exists in isolation. Rather, all texts are made up of references to or quotations from other texts, and are always in conversation with other texts. Intertextuality is not restricted to the idea of one author being influenced or informed by another author, but rather encompasses the idea that each text is engaged with preceding texts. T.S. Eliot's *The Wasteland*, for example, continually quotes from a huge range of literary works and languages, requiring the author's explanatory footnotes; through such intertextuality Eliot engages his readers in networks of ideas and interpretations that are larger than his individual poem. Intertextuality is related to Genette's concept of hypertext.

ISA

ISA, or Ideological State Apparatus, is a term used by Louis Althusser to describe how ideologies are produced and disseminated in a culture. In discussing how any culture gets its people to behave according to its laws, Althusser posits two kinds of State Apparatuses or mechanisms by which the government in power enforces its policies. The first of these is the RSA, or Repressive State Apparatus, which includes the police, the military, and the judicial and prison systems. A person who does not behave correctly can be forcibly detained by an RSA, which has the power to physically confine or punish the wrongdoer. The second is the Ideological State Apparatus, which are the social mechanisms that teach us the right and wrong ways to behave by interpellating us into specific ideologies. Schools, churches, families, political parties, sports, and arts all create a particular worldview or way of thinking about reality, to which individuals either subscribe or do not subscribe. Althusser specifies that these are state apparatuses, meaning that the state, the government, has a stake in dictating what kinds of beliefs are offered within its jurisdiction; the best example of this is public school curricula, which Althusser would argue always supports the interests of the ruling or dominant culture and its ideologies. Ideological State Apparatuses work to get subjects to believe and to act in the state's interests, so that subjects behave properly without the need for the forces of the RSAs.

Jouissance

Jouissance is a French word meaning "enjoyment." It is used specifically in Lacanian psychoanalysis and in post-structural feminist theory in sexual terms, with the connotation of "orgasm" or "coming." *Le jouissance* is an experience that is beyond language or mere pleasure, in these theories; its closest parallel would be the experience of the sublime, which is a combination of ecstasy and terror, according to the Romantics. This experience, which is beyond the aesthetic appreciation of beauty, is terrifying because it threatens the dissolution of the self, the bounded rational ego;

experiences of the sublime are linked to death because both challenge the omnipotence of the existence of the Cartesian self. In Lacanian theory, jouissance is unspeakable, meaning that it is an experience outside the Symbolic realm, not governed by the control of the Phallus. In post-structural feminist theory, jouissance is a distinctively female or feminine experience, a form of sexual pleasure that is disruptive to the phallogocentric Symbolic order and which creates instability and play in language.

Lack

A concept central to Lacanian psychoanalysis. The literal definition of "lack" is to be missing or absent, to not have something. Lacan's idea of lack starts with Freud's assertion that a female lacks a penis, and the trauma that this creates for both boys and girls when they discover this anatomical distinction between the sexes. Freud says that boys automatically see girls as being "castrated," as having had their penis removed; girls, on the other hand, become jealous of the boy's superior organ and understand the innate inferiority of the female sex. For Freud, this paradigm of the presence or absence of the penis plays a central role in the Castration and Oedipus Complexes; boys fear losing their penises, and girls surrender to the inferiority of not having penises. Freud asserts that this castration anxiety forms the basis for the formation of the superego and the unconscious. Lacan translates Freud's literal penis into the Phallus that is the center of the Symbolic Order, or consciousness. For Lacan, the Phallus is a transcendental signified, the ultimate place of power and control, which no human being inhabits or can attain. Lacan argues that all humans are constituted by and as "lack," that no one individual is the source or center of meaning or consciousness. For Lacan, "consciousness" is the ability to say "I" and have that designate something—to be able to speak the signifier of the self or identity. Lacan associates consciousness with the Symbolic Order, with the structure of language, which connects a signifier to a signified to create stable meaning; within the Symbolic Order, the Phallus serves as the center that controls all the units and holds all signifiers in place. The human ability to use language as a stable form of representation—to be able to say a word and have others know what you mean by that word—depends upon our entry into the Symbolic Order, where we agree to follow the rule of the Phallus, which Lacan also calls the Law of the Father or the Name of the Father. When we enter the Symbolic Order, we subject ourselves to the Law of the Father, and acknowledge that we are not the center—that no individual person can occupy the position of the Phallus—and thus acknowledge our "lack." In acknowledging our lack in relation to the Phallus, however, we become subjects in language—we gain the ability to connect signifiers with signifieds to create words that have stable meaning. Our subjecthood thus depends upon our subjection—our ability to speak depends upon our acknowledgement of "lack" in relation to the Phallus.

Freud insisted that males, because they have penises, were associated with presence, and females, due to the lack of penises, were associated with absence. Male/female thus correlates with the binary oppositions presence/absence and complete/incomplete. Lacan argues that no human is fully present or complete, that we are all constituted by and as lack in relation to the Phallus or Law of the Father; in order to speak, in order to have an identity, to say "I", all subjects have to subject themselves to the Phallus. For Lacan, gender distinctions arise from how each sex perceives its "lack"—males have an illusion that their penises align them with the Phallus, while females have little basis for such illusion. Post-structural feminist theorists such as Hélène Cixous use this idea that femininity is associated with lack or absence to argue that women have more play and freedom than do men in the Symbolic Order.

Langue

Langue is the French word that means language. It is used by Ferdinand de Saussure to refer to the system of language, or any signifying system, as a whole. "Langue" is made up of individual units called paroles, which is French for word. PAROLE is any particular individual unit within the signifying system, or any sign (which is made of a signifier and a signified) within the system. A parole is a sign consisting of a signifier connected to a signified; a parole can have meaning by itself, as a sign—the meaning comes from the connection between signifier and signified—or in relation to other signs within the signifying system. An individual parole has meaning—which Saussure calls signification—because it consists of one signifier connected to one signified; a parole has meaning—which Saussure calls value—because it is not any of the other signs within a system. In order to know the value of an individual parole, one must know all the elements in the langue. You can think of langue as being the whole thing, all of language and the entire code or signifying system, and of parole being each of the individual words or signs within that system.

L'ecriture feminine

L'ecriture feminine is a term coined by Hélène Cixous, in *The Laugh of the Medusa* (1976), meaning literally "feminine writing." Using Lacan's ideas that the structure of language is centered by the Phallus, and that language within the Symbolic Order is representational, where a single signifier is connected to a single signified, Cixous argues that the subject position of "woman" or the "feminine" is on the margins of the Symbolic, and thus less firmly anchored and controlled by the Phallus. She traces this back through Lacan and Freud, and the psychoanalytic concept that woman is constituted by and as "lack" because of the lack of a penis. One of the consequences, in Freud's view, of the female lack of a penis is that the female unconscious is less repressed, less radically separated from the consciousness (since the threat of castration, which creates repression, has already been carried out). Because of this, Cixous argues, "woman" has always been in a position of otherness and alterity in Western phallogocentric culture. Using Derrida's idea of play, however, Cixous notes that "woman" is decentered, and therefore freer to move and create. The idea of "l'ecriture feminine" comes from the idea, stemming from Freud, that women are incomprehensible, less moral, less rational than men; Freud calls women "the dark continent," and Cixous uses that as a metaphor to celebrate the lack of control possible over the position of woman in the phallogocentric Symbolic Order. Feminine writing is associated with the Lacanian Real, with the maternal body, which is barred from the Symbolic Order; she associates representational writing with the Symbolic, and non-representational writing with the female and maternal bodies. Feminine writing does not belong exclusively to females, however; Cixous argues that anyone can occupy the marginalized position of "woman" within the Symbolic, and write in l'ecriture feminine from that position. Refusing to define or encode l'ecriture feminine—because to define it would be to limit and imprison it within the logic of Western phallogocentric rationalism—Cixous contradictorily asserts that l'ecriture feminine comes from the female body, and that men can write from that position as well. She describes l'ecriture feminine through a variety of metaphors, including milk, orgasm, honey, and the ocean; she claims that l'ecriture feminine serves as a disruptive and deconstructive force, shaking the security and stability of the phallogocentric Symbolic Order, and therefore allowing more play—in gender, writing, and sexuality—for all language-using subjects.

Libido

Libido comes from the Latin term *libidin* meaning "lust" or "desire." It is the term Freud uses to describe all sexual energy, which for Freud constitutes virtually all human energy. Most broadly, "libido" is the human drive for pleasure, a fundamental instinct that Freud insists is innate in all humans. Certain zones or areas of the body create particularly powerful libidinal pleasure; these include the oral, anal, and phallic (or genital) areas. Freud argues that our first experiences of libido come from the act of sucking, which newborn babies do instinctively in order to survive; Freud asserts that the act of sucking is both life-giving and pleasurable, and it becomes our first awareness of libidinal pleasure. Libido, the drive to feel pleasure, dictates our actions and thoughts from the moment of birth, according to Freud; only as we grow do we begin to learn to subordinate the "pleasure principle," which tells us to satisfy the urges of libido, to the "reality principle," which tells us to delay immediate pleasure for the sake of using our energy to gain something else. Freud calls this process "sublimation," where we learn to redirect libidinal energy towards a goal that is not itself directly pleasurable—to learn to delay sensual gratification in order to accomplish necessary tasks.

Freud says that libido is always an active force, an energy that pushes us to seek pleasure. All pleasure is sexual pleasure, for Freud, and all libidinal energy is active and thus masculine energy. Libidinal energy gets connected to body parts or objects that create pleasure; this is called "cathexis." When libidinal energy gets cathected onto an object, the object becomes the source of pleasure and sexual desire.

Logocentrism

Logocentrism is the name Jacques Derrida gives to the Western philosophical privileging of speech over writing. The Greek word "logos" refers to an ordered rational method of thought that explains the nature or origin of a phenomenon; the ending "-ology" means "the study of" (e.g., psychology means the study of the soul or psyche). Logos often refers to the concept of rational thought, as opposed to desire, which is irrational; it also conjures the idea of the word as representative of the mind's rational processes.

Derrida argues that Western philosophy has always been "logocentric," favoring the spoken word over the written word as the only vehicle for presence, and favoring logic and rationality over irrationality as the only method of finding truth. This logocentrism becomes a powerful form of ethnocentrism, as it privileges the Western phonetic alphabet over other forms of writing, and the tradition of Western logical thought, or science, over other forms of knowing. French psychoanalyst Jacques Lacan and post-structural feminist theorist Hélène Cixous have associated Derrida's logocentrism with the privileging of male and the masculine over female and the feminine with the predominance granted the penis or Phallus in Freudian psychoanalysis, coining the term "Phallogocentric" to encompass all of these meanings.

Marxism

In broad terms, Marxism is the philosophical, economic, and historical ideas and theories articulated by Karl Marx (1818–83), which have become some of the most influential intellectual forces of the twentieth century. Marxist thought has influenced a vast variety of disciplines, including literary studies, history, anthropology, sociology, art, and economics; it has also had a tremendous effect on the forms of social organization developed by nations such as China and the former Soviet Union.

Marxism as an intellectual pursuit can be divided into three main categories: as a philosophy of dialectical materialism, as a mode of understanding history as the result of dialectical materialism, and as a way of understanding economic social formations. As a philosophical school, Marxism follows Hegel in insisting that forces and ideas move through a dialectic, a process of continual formation of thesis, antithesis, and synthesis; the materialist part of dialectical materialism lies in Marxism's insistence that all social beliefs and events have their origins in material culture, in the physical, palpable world of people, their tools, and their work. Dialectical materialism is also a way to think about history, as it explains how events and cultures change through the mechanisms of shifting material practices and the beliefs that accompany them.

Perhaps the most familiar aspect of Marxism, though, is its critique of the capitalist economic system as fundamentally unjust and inhumane. As a materialist, Marx was interested in how any society organizes its production—how people and their tools make the things they need to survive and flourish. He argued that the mode of production of any society was the determining factor in shaping how that society worked—that every aspect of a society could be traced back to the influence of the mode of production. The capitalist mode of production, according to Marx, created a social organization that split the population into owners and workers, and empowered the owners to appropriate the products of the workers' labor power as their property and right. Within capitalism, a worker, or member of the proletariat, is forced to sell his or her labor power for a wage to a company that owns the tools or means of production. The worker takes raw materials and uses tools to create something that can be sold for more than the value of the raw material and the worker's wage; this is called surplus value. The surplus value created by the laborer's work does not belong to the laborer, however, but to the owner of the means of production, who reaps the profit created by the laborer's efforts. For Marxists, this set of social relations produces a fundamental alienation—first, the alienation of the worker from the products of his or her work, and, insofar as the worker has to sell his or her labor power as a commodity, the alienation of the worker from him or herself. This double alienation marks capitalism as a particularly dehumanizing form of economic organization, particularly for the proletariat, who become commodities for owners to purchase. As a political theory, Marxism examines the contradictions and tensions inherent in capitalism's creation of two opposing social classes, and predicts that the collapse of capitalism will follow from the collective power of the working classes uniting to defeat the interests of the owning class.

Méconnaissance

Méconnaissance is the French word meaning "misrecognition" or "misunderstanding." The term comes primarily from Jacques Lacan's post-structural psychoanalysis, and refers to the child's misrecognition of itself in its image in the mirror. The child in the Imaginary phase has no notion of its "self" as a unified being, or of its body being a unified and coordinated whole. At some point, the child sees itself in a mirror, and sees the image of its body as one thing; often there are adults around to reinforce this visual experience of wholeness with the linguistic marker "it's you!" The child then identifies the signifier "I" and the concept of self with the image it sees in the mirror; for Lacan, this is an act of méconnaissance because the visual image is not in fact the child. This misrecognition then is the basis for the child's ego, which Lacan argues is always an illusion produced by seeing itself in the mirror.

Méconnaissance as misunderstanding is also a characteristic of post-structuralist writing and rhetoric, as exemplified in the works of Lacan and Derrida, who purposely use neologisms, puns, and other linguistic devices to make their essays difficult to read. Post-structuralist theorists such as Lacan and Derrida want to call attention to the processes of writing, reading, and interpretation, and thus want their essays to force the reader to be aware of the constructedness of the text and the structures of language being employed. This intentional obfuscation produces *"méconnaissance"*—the (unavoidable) tendency to misunderstand, or misinterpret, what the text says. As Lacan says, to understand is to misunderstand—to think you can use rationality and logic to grasp the truth of a text is to fall back into the logocentric formulations that post-structuralism is trying to question and reject. When you think you understand, you are missing the point; only when you misunderstand, or do not understand, you are thinking as the post-structuralist stylists want you to.

Metaphor and metonymy

They are the two most common tropes or forms of rhetoric used in literary compositions. Metaphor is the creation of an association of similarity and identity between two otherwise unlike objects or ideas: the statement "love is a rose" equates the idea of love with the flower, creating a connection between the two. Metonymy is the creation of an association between things based on closeness or contiguity, or by naming a part of something to indicate the whole: the statement "all hands on deck" substitutes the idea of "hands" as a body part to mean the idea of the whole bodies of sailors.

These two linguistic devices have particular importance in a variety of structuralist and post-structuralist theories. Russian formalist Roman Jakobson insisted that all forms of linguistic representation could be classified as either metaphor or metonymy. Sigmund Freud used the ideas of metaphor and metonymy in his descriptions of condensation and displacement as the two primary mechanisms through which the unconscious encodes information in dreams; post-structural psychoanalyst Jacques Lacan expands on Freud's notion in arguing that the unconscious is structured like a language. Other theorists who explore the importance of metaphor and metonymy include Jacques Derrida, Paul de Man, Paul Ricoeur, and Hayden White.

Mirror stage or mirror phase

The mirror stage is a crucial part of Lacan's version of how a baby becomes a self. In Lacan's version of psychoanalytic theory, human beings start out as undifferentiated blobs—a baby does not know the boundaries of its bodies, does not know the distinction between itself and others, does not know it has a "self" or an identity that is separate from that of its caregivers. Lacan calls this stage of non-differentiation "the Real," where the baby has only needs that can be satisfied. The baby needs food, for instance, and a breast or bottle satisfies that need; the baby-blob does not know that the food comes from an other, or that others exist. Because all the baby's needs can be satisfied in the Real, there is no "lack" or absence—nothing is missing, all is complete and whole and full for the baby. Because there is no lack or absence, according to Lacan, there is no language, no need for representation of something that is not there. Towards the end of the first 6 months of life, the baby moves from the Real to the Imaginary. In this stage, the baby experiences demands that cannot be satisfied by an object. The baby begins to know the concept of "other" in the Imaginary stage—it begins to know that there are things (people, objects) that are not it. The baby has no concept of "self" as yet, but it is aware that there are things that are not under its control. This is the baby's first experience of lack, of otherness. The baby in the Imaginary experiences itself as fragmented; when it sees its own hand, it does not know that the hand belongs to it. The baby has no sense of its body as an integrated, coordinated whole, and has no sense of an integrated self. The baby does, however, see other people as whole, because vision is a sense that happens all at once: when you see something, you see it instantaneously as a whole. So the baby can see that other people (such as its caregivers) are whole beings, with all their body parts connected. It does not yet experience itself as that kind of whole being, however—wholeness belongs to others, until the mirror stage. At some point between 6 and 18 months, according to Lacan, a baby will see itself in a mirror. Someone (usually a caregiver) will say to the baby, "who is that?" and will answer "it's you!" The baby thus learns to associate what it sees in the mirror—a whole integrated body—with the concept of "self," because the baby is told that the image in the mirror is the baby. What the baby sees is a whole body, not a fragmented, disjointed one. The baby misrecognizes itself as what it sees in the mirror. The mirror image is only an image, however; it is not the baby itself. The baby learns then to associate an image of wholeness with the idea of "self" and to designate that self with the signifier "I." For Lacan, the mirror stage is the gateway to the Symbolic Order, to the ability to use signifiers to represent concepts to create stable understandable meaning. The mirror image then becomes the basis for the baby's sense of ego or self, a misrecognition of itself as whole, complete, and powerful, rather than as subject to the Law of the Father in the Symbolic Order.

Monologia

Monologia is a term associated with Mikhail Bakhtin's discussion of the social patterns of speech; it is the opposite of "dialogic." Monologia is speaking with a single voice, rather than entering into a dialogue, an exchange of ideas; a monologue is spoken by a single character who is onstage by himself, not speaking directly to anyone else. Bakhtin describes monologia as the voice of a central authority making pronouncements that cannot be questioned or debated; monologia is thus a tool of repression. The movements toward establishing a single correct language, such as English-only, or even the efforts to enforce a standard of correct language usage, are examples of monologia. The professor who corrects your grammar is adhering to a monologic doctrine.

Mytheme

Mytheme is the name that Claude Lévi-Strauss gives to the smallest comprehensible unit of the myth in his essay "The Structural Study of Myth"(1955), in which he describes the structural analysis of mythology. It is analogous to phoneme, the smallest identifiable unit of sound; morpheme, the smallest identifiable lexical unit; and sememe, the smallest identifiable signifying unit. A mytheme is a structural unit of the myth and should not be confused with an element of content, like a character; a mytheme is a function within a myth. An example of a mytheme would be the position of " hero," which stands in opposition to the position of "villain" or "enemy." The specific identity of a particular mytheme, such as the name of a specific hero and villain, can vary according to the myth being examined, but the relation between the two mythemes ("heroes" oppose "villains") remains structurally the same in all myths that use this particular mythemic binary opposition.

Narratology

Narratology is, literally, the science of narrative; narratological theories examine stories and storytelling. Historically, narratology begins with Aristotle's assertion in the *Poetics* that stories can be told in two ways: through a narrator or *diagesis*, and through showing the actions of characters or *mimesis*. The rise of the novel as dominant narrative form, beginning in the eighteenth century in the West, favored mimetic representation; stories were best when they seemed realistic, without the interruption of a narrator. This method of narration promoted the use of free indirect discourse, where the thoughts and actions of characters were presented without direct mediation, as in third-person omniscient narration. The rise of structuralism in the 1960s directed new attention to theories of narrative, such as Claude Levi-Strauss' studies of mythology. Structuralist narratology identified two basic elements of all stories: the story, or the semantic structure that existed independent of any medium, and the discourse, the verbal or visual presentation of this structure. Story and discourse are thus similar to Saussure's *langue* and *parole*, indicating the totality of the structure and individual instances that fill the structure. Structuralist narratologists include Levi-Strauss, Tzvetan Todorov, A. J. Greimas, and Gerard Genette. Roland Barthes, in *S/Z*, discusses the narrative codes that shape meaning in a Balzac short story. Post-structural narratologists, such as Mikhail Bakhtin, discuss narrative as polyvocal or heteroglossic employing a variety of different sociolects or rhetorics, as opposed to the unitary voice of poetry celebrated by New Criticism. Post-structuralist narratology, drawing on ideas from Marxism, speech act theory, psychoanalysis, and feminist theory, also argues that narratives produce consciousness and reality rather than merely reflecting them. Many narratologists, such as Hayden White and Teresa de Lauretis, emphasize the political ramifications of narratives in shaping ideologies and practices.

New criticism

New Criticism is the name given to the formalist movement in Anglo-American literary studies that emphasized studying the literary text in isolation without regard for anything external to the text, like history, psychology, or biography. Associated with critics such as F. R. Leavis, Cleanth Brooks, and John Crowe Ransom, New Criticism became the dominant method of literary studies in universities from the 1940s through the 1960s. The principles of New Criticism were first articulated in the 1920s by T. S. Eliot, who argued that critics must focus on the poem not on the poet. According to critic I. A. Richards, the main principles of New Criticism included the autonomy of the work of art, its resistance to paraphrase, its organic unity, and the need for the method of study known as "close reading." New Criticism gained authority in university systems in England and the United States after World War II, as an effort to make literary studies more objective like the sciences. Like Russian formalism and structuralism, New Criticism rejected political and historical methods of literary analysis; though they argued against any emotionally informed reading of the text, New Critics like Richards did emphasize the emotive function of language, in opposition to its referential function. This method proved more applicable to poetry than to other literary forms, as many critics of New Criticism have pointed out; it also viewed a literary work as a naturally occurring object, similar to objects of scientific study rather than the product of specifically human conscious effort. New Criticism's emphasis on the possibility of objectivity in close reading served to validate literary studies as the equivalent of the sciences, rather than as the articulation of individual perceptions and emotions. It had the additional benefit of accommodating the heterogeneous population of college students who flooded universities after the war; students with no particular historical or classical background could approach any work of literature with only the literary text and a dictionary to work with. New Criticism came to be discredited with the advent of socially conscious forms of literary study in the 1960s, and with the predominance of poststructuralist theories later in the twentieth century. However, the New Critical insistence on close reading, the meticulous examination of the meaning and connotations of the words used in a text, remains a fundamental method for all literary studies.

New historicism

New Historicism is the name given to interdisciplinary historical cultural studies. New Historicism first appeared in Renaissance

Studies, and was associated with Stephen Greenblatt. New Historicism rejects the compartmentalization of disciplines fostered by the university system, insisting that a particular cultural moment or phenomenon can best be understood through examination of multiple factors, including economic, political, literary, religious, and aesthetic beliefs and practices. Not a school, doctrine, or methodology, New Historicism, also called "cultural poetics," insists that all forms of discourse interact with all other forms of discourse; it shares with Michel Foucault and Louis Althusser the insistence that all institutional and individual practices are informed by discourse and ideology. A full analysis of a cultural phenomenon thus requires what anthropologist Clifford Geertz calls "thick description": the close reading of the rhetoric of texts and practices from all aspects of a culture. New Historicists also insist that the writer be self-reflexive, making it clear that interpretations come from a specific scholar and perspective rather than presenting "truth."

Objet petit a

A French phrase meaning literally "object small a." The phrase refers to a concept from Lacanian psychoanalysis concerning the idea of "other" or "*autre*" in French. The small a "*autre*" or small o "other" designates the other first perceived by the infant during the Imaginary phase, when the baby becomes aware that there are people and objects beyond its control and awareness. While the baby does not yet have a sense of "self" or "I," it grasps the idea of "otherness" through its interactions with a "small o other," which is not the baby itself. This leads to the phase of demand, which cannot be satisfied. Demand is Lacan's term for the baby's insistence that the knowledge of "otherness" cease to exist; the baby wants to return to the sense of wholeness and unity it had in the Real. Thus "o"therness is a stepping stone to desire, as the baby will experience it in the Symbolic Realm; desire is the desire to be or to have the Other, to be or have the Phallus, the center of the Symbolic. The small o "other" is the baby's first experience of the structuring power of the Other, which will dominate its sense of self, its "I"dentity, and its use of language and consciousness within the Symbolic.

Oedipus

In Greek mythology, Oedipus is the son of King Laius and Queen Jocasta of Thebes, who is prophesied at birth to grow to kill his father and marry his mother. To avoid this fate, his parents abandon Oedipus on a mountainside and leave him crippled, in the hope that he will die. He survives, however, without knowing his true identity, and does grow up to kill his father and marry his mother; upon learning the truth, Oedipus puts out his own eyes in remorse. The story is told in tragedies by Aeschylus, Sophocles, and others.

The Oedipus myth plays a centrally important role in Freudian psychoanalysis, as Freud saw the desire to kill the father to obtain sole sexual possession of the mother as the root and basis of all human sexuality. For Freud, all babies begin by having a libidinal cathexis to their mothers, who, as the primary caregivers, first introduce the baby to erotic sensation. The baby then comes to associate pleasure with the mother's body, via breastfeeding, diaper changing, washing, etc., and directs its libidinal sexual drives towards the mother—the baby wants the mother for itself, so that the mother will continue creating the pleasurable feelings the baby wants. Eventually, however, the baby learns that the mother's body and its pleasures belong to someone else—to the father, who takes the mother away from the baby. The baby then enters into what Freud calls the Oedipus Complex, where it wants to kill its father to get sole possession of its mother and the pleasure her body provides.

According to Freud, the Oedipus Complex was a cultural universal—every child in every culture, he claimed, goes through a version of the Oedipus Complex on the path to adult sexuality. The Oedipus Complex explained, for Freud, why a "normal" human desired someone of the opposite sex: boys wanted to kill their fathers to marry their mothers, and girls supposedly wanted to kill their mothers to marry their fathers. In Freud's view, adult reproductive, non-incestuous heterosexuality stems from the correct resolution of the Oedipus Complex. For boys, this resolution comes via the Castration Complex. A boy sees a girl naked for the first time, and realizes she does not have a penis. He believes that she used to have one, but that the father cut off her penis, probably because she was touching her penis while having libidinal thoughts about the mother. The boy then becomes afraid that the father will cut off his penis also if he continues to associate his phallic pleasure with his mother. Fear of castration forces the boy to repress his desire for his mother into his unconscious, and to store his obedience to his father's power in his superego or conscience. If the boy successfully negotiates the creation of the unconscious and the superego, the father promises that the boy will eventually get a woman of his own with whom to be sexual, thus guaranteeing non-incestuous heterosexuality.

For girls, the Oedipus Complex works differently. Like a boy, a girl wants to have her mother and the sexual pleasure her mother creates in care-giving; like the boy, the girl becomes aware that the father has a prior claim on the mother and her pleasures. Like the boy, the girl's pleasure is active and "phallic," as Freud does not distinguish between penis and clitoris. The girl, however, when she sees a boy naked for the first time, recognizes instantly that she does not have a penis, and knows instantly that she is inferior because of that lack; according to Freud, the girl is already castrated. She can then accept "the fact" of her castration, and begin to hate her mother (and all women) for not having the superior organ and for not giving her a penis, and desire to get a penis through the father, by intercourse or by having a male baby. This creates the necessary non-incestuous heterosexual orientation that Freud decreed "normal." The girl wants to kill her mother and marry her father.

Problems arise with this formulation, however, as the Oedipus Complex works better for boys than for girls. If girls are already castrated, what motivation do they have to give up their incestuous desires and create a superego and unconscious? Freud ultimately cannot explain the female version of the Oedipus Complex, which he at various times called the Electra Complex and the negative Oedipus Complex.

That Oedipus becomes blind, putting out his own eyes in grief and remorse for his actions, also has significance in psychoanalytic theory. The basis of sexual difference is the visual presence or absence of the penis, where women are defined as having "nothing to see" and therefore as lacking, while men are defined as having a fully visible and present organ. The realm of the visual, or the scopic, plays a central role in Lacan's version of psychoanalysis, where sexual difference, power, and desire are all oriented around vision or the gaze.

Orientalism

As described by postcolonial theorist Edward Said, Orientalism is the process of making something or someone "oriental." Like Foucault, Said describes this as a discursive process—Western European explorers went to a place they called "the Orient" and wrote descriptions of what they found there; Western European readers read these descriptions and understood "the Orient" as something other than their own country and civilization.

"Orient" in English means "East." "East" and "West" are relative terms, not absolutes; they require a fixed position to have meaning. In the colonial era, this fixed position was Greenwich, England, the home port of the British Royal Navy; zero degrees latitude runs through Greenwich, and "East" and "West" are understood from that reference point.

Said talks about how "the West" constructed "the East" through discourse, where the colonizer produces the writing and the colonized is silent; the colonized people do not produce knowledge, but are only the subject of knowledge produced by the colonizer. When "the West" writes "the East," the writings create the "oriental" as fundamentally "other." The negative binary opposite of "civilization"—sexual exoticism, drug use, immorality, lack of organization, ignorance, poverty—is associated with the "oriental" in this construction.

Other

The term "other" is used in a variety of critical theories, including postcolonial theory, to designate the opposite of the term "self" or "subject" as it is understood in Western philosophy. A "self" has a number of distinct characteristics in Western/humanist philosophy, including the capacity for reason, self-reflection, the ability to speak and to say "I," individuality, autonomy, and self-determination. The "other," as the binary opposite of "self," lacks these characteristics; in the logic of binary oppositions, the "other" is everything the self is not. When the self is defined as white, male, free, literate, and normal, the "other" thus stands for non-white, female, enslaved, illiterate, and abnormal. The creation of "other" is necessary to the maintenance of the category "self" as bounded and stable. Other, with a capital "O," is used in psychoanalytic theory to refer to the structural position of the center in the Symbolic Order, which Lacan also calls the Phallus, The Name of the Father, or the Law of the Father. Following a Hegelian dialectical model found in the relations between master and slave, Lacan locates the Other as the place of desire; a person's desire is always the desire of the Other, the desire to be the Other, to eliminate the distinction between "self" and "other" on the structural or phenomenological level. Speech, according to Lacan, originates in the Other, in the Symbolic Order to which the individual speaking subject must subject itself; the Other is the center of the Symbolic, always something beyond the self, the ego, the "I"dentity.

Overdetermination

A term used in both psychoanalytic and Marxist theories, overdetermination in general describes a phenomenon that cannot be attributed to a single or unitary causal factor. Freud discussed overdetermination in discussing dream analysis: a theme may appear in multiple ways or forms in a patient's dream life, and cannot thus be linked to a single unconscious cause. Louis Althusser discusses overdetermination as a way of critiquing the classic Marxist assumption that the economic base determines what happens in a society's superstructure. For Althusser, economic relations help to determine ideological beliefs but are not the sole or only factor in that determination. Rather, a cultural belief is determined by some aspect of the economic system and by an individual's life experience, and by the specific mechanism by which that belief is articulated—any belief is thus overdetermined by multiple factors and cannot be traced to a single cause.

Panopticon

Panopticon is a term associated with Michel Foucault's discussion of surveillance and discipline in *Discipline and Punish*. The panopticon was British utilitarian philosopher Jeremy Bentham's design for a modern prison, which consisted of a central tower around which were a ring of cells; the interior of each cell could be seen from the tower, but the interior of the tower could not be seen from any cell. This meant that prisoners did not know when they were being watched and when they were not, and had thus to assume that their behavior was always being monitored; it also meant that there could be few or no guards in the tower, since the prisoners had no way of knowing who might be watching them. Foucault uses the idea of the panopticon to discuss how subjects in contemporary culture are self-regulating and self-disciplined; we behave as if we are always under surveillance, because we never know when we are being watched. Foucault discusses panopticism as the characteristic form of discipline in modern societies, where subjects internalize their own sense of being constantly visible to authority. The ubiquity of surveillance cameras everywhere in Western culture supports Foucault's ideas; the operations of power deployed through panopticism are met with subjects' efforts to become invisible, to remain unseen. Examples of such games appear frequently in popular movies and fiction, particularly those, like Mission Impossible, that present situations of espionage and security.

Parole

Parole is any particular individual unit within the signifying system, or any sign (which is made of a signifier and a signified) within the system. A parole is a sign consisting of a signifier connected to a signified; a parole can have meaning by itself, as a sign—the meaning comes from the connection between signifier and signified—or in relation to other signs within the signifying system. An individual parole has meaning—which Saussure calls signification—because it consists of one signifier connected to one signified; a parole has meaning—which Saussure calls value—because it is none of the other signs within a system. In order to know the value of an individual parole, one must know all the elements in the langue. You can think of the langue as being the whole thing, all of language, the entire code or signifying system, and of parole being each of the individual words or signs within that system.

Penis envy

Penis envy is a concept associated with Freudian psychoanalysis, asserting that the penis is the only sexual organ and the most valuable one. In his theories about the Oedipus and Castration Complexes, Freud argued that the visibility of the penis made it superior to any other sexual organ; the clitoris and vagina are inferior to the penis because they are not visible in a commonplace nude (i.e. a naked person standing upright and viewed from the front). In describing the reaction of each sex to seeing the other sex naked, Freud proclaimed that a boy on first seeing a naked girl immediately thinks her penis has been cut off; a girl on seeing a naked boy, immediately thinks the same. Both boys and girls innately attribute the penis with organ superiority and respond accordingly, classifying beings with penises as vastly superior to beings without penises.

The boy's response to seeing the penis-less girl is to fear castration, and thus to create an unconscious and a superego; the girl's response to her lack of penis is to feel jealousy and envy of the superior organ, to feel herself to be inherently inferior, and to want to get a penis of her own. Feminist theorists point out that Freud's assumption of the superiority of the penis is a prime example of the patriarchal bias of psychoanalytic theory; penis envy has been used widely as an explanation for why women might want any form of equality with men.

Phallocentric

Phallocentric refers to any system that is centered around the phallus, or which gives primacy to the penis. Freudian psychoanalysis is a phallocentric system because Freud asserts that the penis is the only visible and valuable sexual organ; possession or lack of a penis is crucial to his formulation of the Oedipus and Castration Complexes, which in turn form the basis of his theory of the ego, unconscious, and superego.

Phallogocentric

Phallogocentric refers to a combination of phallocentric and logocentric systems of thought. Jacques Derrida describes Western metaphysics as logocentric, centered on logic and on the spoken word as guarantor of presence and identity. An example of logocentrism is the Biblical account of the creation of the world: "In the Beginning was the Word." From a logocentric perspective, speech is the original form of language and writing is merely the transcription of speech; the power of speech is associated with consciousness, selfhood, and rational thought. Jacques Derrida's deconstruction is a critique of this philosophical stance. He accuses Jacques Lacan of being both phallocentric, in naming the Phallus as the center of the Symbolic Order, and logocentric, in naming the Phallus as the source and origin of language, the transcendental signified, and names this stance "phallogocentrism." Hélène Cixous and post-structural feminists also critique phallogocentric Western philosophy for its subordination of the feminine to the masculine.

Phallus

Phallus is sometimes used as a synonym for "penis." In Lacanian psychoanalysis the Phallus is the name given to the center of the Symbolic Order, the structural position that governs all of the elements of the Order. Insofar as the Symbolic Order is the structure of language itself, where subjects are able to connect signifiers and signifieds in order to achieve stable meaning, language is a *phallocentric* system, centered on the Phallus as the organizing and ruling power. Lacan names this center "the Phallus" to pay tribute to Freud's assertion that the penis is the only visible and valuable organ; the Phallus is the ultimate position and source of power. While the penis is a literal organ, however, the Phallus is symbolic—no one individual, male or female, has the Phallus or can occupy the position of the Phallus. The Phallus conjures the idea of the father, whose threat of castration forces the boy into repressing his Oedipal desires for his mother to create an unconscious, and into creating a superego or conscience in which the father's voice is internalized as the voice of authority and law. Lacan also refers to the Phallus as the Name of the Father and the Law of the Father for this reason.

Play

Play in a post-structuralist context means the same thing it does in an engineering or architectural context: the amount of movement possessed by any particular element of a system or structure. In buildings, play is limited: most office towers, for example, will "play" in a high wind or during an earthquake so that they are not so rigid as to break apart when facing an external force. Play in post-structuralism means the freedom of movement or flexibility of a system or of its elements; the center of a system governs the amount of play available. Play in a linguistic or signifying system is the ability of one sign to have multiple meanings, or for one signifier to have more than one signified. Play in literary studies is called ambiguity or multiplicity of meaning.

Postcolonial

Postcolonial means "after" colonialism. Generally, the term refers to the period after a former colony gains its independence: India became postcolonial in 1948, when it became a nation of its own and ceased being a colony of the British Empire. But "postcolonial" refers to more than just the establishment of an independent government. Colonialism exists as ideologies and practices that assume the dominance or rightness of the colonizing culture; these ideologies and practices do not end when the colonists leave. Rather, "postcolonial" may refer best to the time period when a previously colonized culture wrestles with the meaning of its identity as an independent entity. What language will a postcolonial society speak—that of the colonizers, which had been the official language, or any indigenous languages? How will the history of the postcolonial nation be taught in their schools or in the schools of the colonizing country? Much postcolonial literary theory examines how authors deal with the issues and contradictions of life in formerly colonized cultures.

Postmodernism

Postmodernism is a complicated term, or set of ideas, that is relatively coterminous with post-structuralism and deconstruction; like all "post"- designations, postmodernism refers to phenomena or ideas that come *after* modernism. Like most "post"- designations, however, this does not help locate it temporally or historically, since it is not clear when "modernism" ends and "postmodernism" begins. Some of the difficulties with the term come from its interdisciplinarity: postmodernism is a concept that appears in a wide variety of fields, including art, architecture, music, film, literature, sociology, communications, fashion, and technology, each of which has a different history and thus a different way of marking the transition between the modern and the postmodern.

Sticking with the literary tradition, we might contrast postmodernism with literary modernism, the movement in the first half of the twentieth century most associated with T. S. Eliot, Virginia Woolf, William Faulkner, Marcel Proust, and Franz Kafka (among others). Modernism saw and represented the world as fragmented and incoherent, as an irrational collection of random events, and lamented the loss of meaning and structure in the modern world. Postmodernism sees the same incoherence but celebrates the ridiculousness of trying to make meaning and order out of the irrational and random; Kurt Vonnegut is an example of this kind of postmodern literary perspective.

In a wider sense, though, postmodern is not what comes after modernism as an aesthetic movement, but rather what comes after "modernity" as a cultural, historical, and philosophical movement. Modernity is the broader term; modernism happens within modernity. Modernity is also the older term; it was used in sociology and history in the nineteenth century to distinguish the current epoch from antiquity or the ancient world. Generally, modernity corresponds to the European Enlightenment, or the Age of Reason, which begins roughly in the middle of the eighteenth century. Modernity, Enlightenment philosophy, and humanism all share some common assumptions, including the idea that there is a stable, coherent, knowable "self" that is conscious, essential, and universal, and the idea that reason is the highest form of mental functioning, which enables an individual self to formulate objective truths, called "science," about how the world works.

In Western Enlightenment philosophy, modernity depends on the structure of the binary opposition: the self exists because there is a concept of non-self, and reason exists because there is a concept of non-reason or madness. One of the fundamental binaries that underlie modernity, according to postmodern theorist Jean-François Lyotard, is order/chaos. Modernity loves order, and sets up systems to create order and banish chaos; anything labeled as "disorder" is labeled disruptive and dangerous, and requires systems of control. Of course, as in all binary systems, the category "disorder" is necessary for the category of "order" to exist; it is thus impossible ever to eliminate disorder to create an entirely ordered society. Rather, modern society continues to create ever-greater categories of disorder to conquer. These categories of order and disorder, according to Lyotard, are maintained by "grand narratives" that explain why certain practices and ideas belong to "order" and others to "disorder." A grand narrative appears as the fundamental truth that underlies any classification of phenomena into a binary system that values one term over another. Postmodernism, then, is the deconstruction of the binary systems that underlie modernity, and a skepticism and questioning of the grand narratives that support those binary systems.

One more aspect of modernity and postmodernity worth consideration here is that of language. In Enlightenment modern thought, language is a transparent medium for the conveyance of ideas; words serve only to represent thoughts or things and do not have any function or power beyond that. Within this framework, signifiers always point to signifieds—meaning resides in the signified, in the idea or thing being represented in language rather than in the words or signifiers themselves, because reality exists within the signifieds. In postmodernism, however, language is itself constructive rather than simply a medium; signification creates reality rather than just reflecting or naming it. Further, the power of signifiers to create meaning precludes the possibility of signifieds—in a postmodern world, there are only signifiers, only surfaces, with nothing beyond.

Post-structuralism

Post-structuralism is an "umbrella" term that refers to the ways of thinking about human thought and culture that developed in the 1970s as a response to and criticism of humanist and structuralist thought. Though post-structuralist ideas occur in a wide variety of contexts and disciplines, most have a shared set of ideas and values that include the following:

- The "self" is a constructed entity, not an essential core of being. A self is fluid; its markers of identity, including race, gender, sex, and sexuality, are all socially constructed and therefore unstable and changeable.

- The "self" and its experiences are all products of language; we don't speak language, language speaks us. All human consciousness of the external world is created by language and cannot exist without it. Reality is thus the product of language.

- There is no distinction between the "self" and the external world, as both are constructed by language itself, and hence there can be no objective mode of knowledge; without objectivity, there is no such thing as a universal truth. Rather, truth itself is constructed, and therefore mutable.

- What is called truth or science or fact is the product of ideology: belief systems that are articulated within a culture and which individuals inhabit; ideology determines all human thought and practice.

Power/knowledge

This phrase is associated specifically with Michel Foucault's later genealogical works, where he examines how discursive and non-discursive formations weave together networks of power and knowledge that define the human subject in various ways. The slash between the two does not signify a binary opposition, as in male/female, but rather a necessary linkage between the two concepts: a paraphrase might be "knowledge is power and power is knowledge." Foucault argues that discourses create forms of knowledge that shape social practices; the practices then enmesh subjects (people) into relations of power. An example might be the university, which is divided up into various departments—literature, history, biology, psychology, sociology. Each department produces its own particular kind of knowledge, and each kind of knowledge produces a particular way of thinking about and acting in the world. A psychologist, for example, creates and produces knowledge about how the human mind works; this knowledge is then put into practice in psychotherapy, in hospitals and rehab programs, funded by insurance companies (or not), and written about and taught in college classrooms.

Psychoanalysis

Psychoanalysis is a science of the human mind pioneered and articulated by Sigmund Freud at the turn of the nineteenth century. As a medical doctor, Freud was interested in finding cures for human suffering; he charted the source of much suffering to psychological rather than physiological or biological causes. In his explorations of the relationship between mind and body, Freud posited that thoughts could directly cause physical symptoms that had no physiological cause. His efforts to chart the mechanisms by which the mind affected the body led to his articulation and development of psychoanalysis. Psychoanalysis is the broad term given to the theories developed by Freud and by his followers, including Jungian psychoanalysis, Kleinian psychoanalysis, ego psychology, object–relations theory, and Lacanian psychoanalysis.

Freud's theories of psychoanalysis were constantly evolving and transforming during his lifetime, and have gone in a vast variety of directions since. All schools of psychoanalytic thought share some basic characteristics and assumptions, including the idea of the *unconscious* as a realm of thought inaccessible to the conscious rational mind, and the idea that the contents of the unconscious can be accessed, interpreted, and analysed. Thoughts that are repellent to or unacceptable to the conscious mind are repressed into the unconscious, where psychic energy is used to imprison them; most psychoanalysts hold that the energy used to repress unacceptable thoughts causes forms of mental distress or illness, such as neurosis and psychosis. The therapeutic goal of most schools of psychoanalysis, following Freud, is to make the conscious mind aware of the contents of the unconscious so that less energy is required for repression; the primary mode for uncovering the contents of the unconscious is *analysis*, in which the patient works to put into words the thoughts being repressed. Classical psychoanalysis as therapy involves frequent sessions with a trained analyst, where the patient tries to articulate censored thoughts and, through the mechanism of transference, project these onto the analyst. Virtually all psychotherapy in our contemporary world can trace its roots back to some aspect of Freudian psychoanalysis.

Queer

The dictionary definition of "queer" is peculiar, odd, strange, or different from the norm. In popular usage, "queer" is often synonymous with "gay," in part because "queer" was a pejorative term for homosexuals in the first half of the twentieth century. In critical theory, however, the word "queer" points to a specific mode of thinking about sexuality that goes beyond the binary categories of homosexual and heterosexual. Following the deconstructive practices of post-structuralist theory, "queer" at the end of the twentieth century takes on the meaning of disruptive, destabilizing performances of gender and sexuality, which are not the product of any kind of essentialist identity. To be "gender-queer" is to enact or encode heterogeneous gender signifiers, such as a bearded man wearing a dress; to be sexually "queer" is to enact sexual desires without regard for a consistent notion of a singular sexuality. In this sense, "queer" harkens back to its original meaning, something strange or different. Queer theorists insist, however, that "queer" must always have some component of estrangement related to gender or sexuality (or both).

Race

The dictionary defines "race" as "any of the major divisions of humankind having distinct physical characteristics" and as "any category, breed, or variety" of humans. Western thought has focused for centuries on dividing human beings into specific "races," which in the extreme become like different species, and on creating hierarchies of intelligence and worth based on these ideas of "race." Any geography or world history textbook from the nineteenth century or before outlines the "great races of man," dividing the world's population into the Caucasian, the Negro, the Asian, the Indian, etc. Racial classification was the basis for colonialism, for slavery and segregation in the United States, for the Nazi effort to exterminate Jews, and for South African Apartheid. Yet twenty-first-century-science, examining genetics and DNA, have proven that "race" does not exist—the genetic makeup of all humans is fundamentally the same. The physical differences that constituted "race" are not biological givens but rather sets of cultural signifiers. Race is thus a constructed set of ideas and practices, wherein skin color, hair texture, eye shape, and other physical markers are linked with ideologies of behavior, social role, and human capacity. Within a racist system like American slavery, black skin denoted mental and moral inferiority while white skin marked the bearer as superior, therefore rightfully dominating and controlling those with black skin. Slavery and colonialism (to name but two) were built on the insistence that race was a biological truth rather than a socially constructed system; like most such dualistic thought, the truth of "race" can be deconstructed as more and more people, coming from "hybrid" parentage, can no longer be classified as belonging definitively to one "race." Still, the concept of "race" holds enormous power in the twenty-first-century world.

Reader-response theory

Reader-response theory stems from hermeneutics; it is the study of how readers respond to literary and cultural texts. Reader-response theory, or reception theory, emerged as a reaction against the New Critical insistence that all meaning was contained entirely within the text alone without regard for any external factors. Reader-response theorists argue that reading, making meaning, is an active process not a passive one; readers engage with texts and form interpretations based on subjective experiences as well as on what the text says. Some branches of reader-response theory examine individual reader's responses, often from a psychological or psychoanalytic perspective; others look for the social parameters within which interpretation takes place, arguing that "interpretive communities" establish particular modes of reading. Theorists associated with reader-response theory include Wolfgang Iser, Stanley Fish, E. D. Hirsch, and David Bleich.

Real

The Real is the term used by Lacan to designate the original ground of being, the first state of human awareness into which all of us are born. The Real is defined as a state of being wherein the infant has no perception of itself as a separate individual person; rather, in the Real, the infant is aware only of its needs and the satisfaction of those needs. A baby is hungry and it gets fed; it is dirty and gets a diaper change. In Lacanian psychoanalysis, a baby in the Real has no idea where its care is coming from, or that any person is caring for it; it knows only needs and the satisfaction of needs. Because of this, there is no lack or absence—everything the baby needs is supplied to it and the baby knows only two states of being: need and fullness. In the Real, there is no language or need for representation or symbolism because what the baby needs is always there. The baby thus has no language and no sense of self or identity; it experiences only completion and fullness and union with its caregivers. The Real must be abandoned in order for the baby to become a language-using speaking subject; as with most psychoanalytic theories, the Real represents a kind of original paradise that must be left in order to become a separate individual. The Real is beyond representation and thus beyond the Symbolic Order; in Lacan's trajectory, the Real is prior to the Symbolic and thus poses a threat to the stability of the Symbolic Order. The Real in feminist theory is often associated with the maternal body, which must be renounced in order to gain entry to language in the Symbolic Order; the Phallus as center of the Symbolic is thus established against, and in fear of, the realm of the Real.

Rhizome

Rhizome comes from the Greek *rhizoma*. Rhizome is often taken as being synonymous with "root"; in botany, a rhizome is a plant structure that grows underground and has both roots (commonly, the part that grows down into the ground) and shoots (commonly, the part that grows up through the ground). The word is associated with postmodern theorists Gilles Deleuze and Felix Guattari, who use the rhizome to describe a process of existence and growth that does not come from a single central point of origin. In *A Thousand Plateuas*, Deleuze and Guattari name *arborescence* or the model of the tree as the paradigm for knowledge and practice in the modern Western world; in this model, a small idea—a seed or acorn—takes root and grows into a tree with a sturdy trunk supporting numerous branches, all linked to and traceable back to the original seed. The seed or acorn thus is the beginning point of a coherent organic system that grows vertically and progressively, continually sending out branches that are part of, and identical to, the point of origin. This arborescence, they argue, is the way Western logic and philosophy has worked: in this case, Plato might be the seed and all subsequent philosophies are outgrowths of Platonic thought.

In the postmodern world, however, Deleuze and Guattari argue, the grand narrative of arborescence falls apart. They offer instead the rhizome or fungus, which is an organism of interconnected living fibers that has no central point, no origin, and no particular form or unity or structure. A rhizome does not start from anywhere or end anywhere; it grows from everywhere, and is the same at any point. As such, a rhizome has no center, which makes it difficult to uproot or destroy; you might think of a mold or fungus, which can reproduce from any cell. Postmodern culture resembles this rhizome more than the tree, according to Deleuze and Guattari. An example of this might be the internet, the World Wide Web, which has a rhizomatic structure. It has no point of origin, no central locus, nothing that controls or shapes or organizes it: the web simply grows. You can take out any link or any website (even any web browser) without damaging or changing the internet—it continues to exist without path or pattern.

Self

A concept central to Enlightenment and humanist philosophies about human beings, a "self" is what we name when we say "I" or "me." This self has a number of specific traits in Western thought including the capacity for rational thought, language and self-representation, self-reflection, and the ability to think objectively to discover truth. This self is understood as something unique to every individual yet also containing elements that are universal, that all selves have in common. The self is a constant, unchanging core of identity, which has distinct boundaries and remains essentially the same regardless of external circumstances: no matter what happens, I will always be me. Because of this essential core of identity, the self is autonomous and independent, able to create its own meanings and make its own decisions; it exists, in philosophies from Descartes on, as an isolated bounded sovereign entity. "Self" exists as the positive term in the binary opposition "self/other," where "other" designates everything that is not "self," not "me," therefore not fully human.

In post-structuralist theories, the concept of the Cartesian self is challenged by the concept of "subject," a being created by and in language. The subject lacks the autonomy and authority of the self; a subject is always subjected to rules and authorities greater than itself.

Semiology

Ferdinand do Saussure defined semiology as the science of signs or the study of how signs operate in the social world. Like his structural linguistics, semiology investigates the rules that govern how signs are put together to create meaning. Roland Barthes expands Saussure's idea of semiology in his *Elements of Semiology* (1964) to include any system of signs, not just linguistic ones. In *Mythologies* (1973) Barthes argues that almost any cultural event or production can be studied semiologically, and investigates fashion, menus, advertising, and other everyday examples of signs conveying meaning.

Semiotic

As defined by Julia Kristeva, the "semiotic" is the realm that comes before Lacan's Symbolic Order in the development of the human linguistic consciousness. From the Greek *semeion*, meaning "trace" or "sign," the semiotic is associated with the maternal body and with what Lacan calls the Real, which are repressed and unrepresentable in the Symbolic. The semiotic is a layer of libidinal energy that is disruptive to the Symbolic, and to the logic and grammar of stable language; similar to Cixous' *l'ecriture femi-nine*, the semiotic is an expression of libidinal desire unmapped and unconfined by the Law of the Father. Though developmentally linked to the maternal body, the semiotic can be inhabited by persons of any sex; the languages produced from the semiotic are poetic and transgressive.

Semiotics

Semiotics is synonymous with semiology. Some definitions emphasize that semiotics comes from an American branch of the study of signs stemming from the works of C. S. Peirce, a late-nineteenth-century Harvard philosopher. By the 1970s many writers and theorists preferred the term semiotics because it was less tied to a Western philosophical tradition based on the idea of logos.

Sexuality

Since the end of the nineteenth century, sexuality has been considered one of the primary elements in a person's essential identity along with race, class, and gender; in this view, one is born into an unchanging sexuality that forms a central core of how one identifies oneself and acts in the world. The idea of "sexuality" as a concept was produced by medical and psychiatric discourses, according to Michel Foucault's *History of Sexuality*. Prior to the articulation of sexuality as a category of identity, sexual acts were only something a person did, not a result or sign of who that person was. People had sex but not sexuality. Sexual acts were classified as transgressive or licit, often with regard to their reproductive function within civil and religious-sanctioned marriage, but the person who committed these acts had no specific sexual identity. The emergence of categories of sexual activity as identity formations created our contemporary understanding of "homosexual" and "heterosexual." These labels have been mapped onto existing binary structures of normality and abnormality, so that "homosexuality" has been synonymous with sickness, deviance, and sin in the languages of medicine, social sciences, and religion.

Western culture in the twentieth century has been obsessed with constructing, analysing, discussing, articulating, and debating questions of sexuality: Is it innate or learned? Can it be changed? Are some forms more acceptable than others? How should unacceptable forms be treated or punished? The creation of vast fields of knowledge concerning sexuality and the continual negotiations of power around sexuality have resulted in both increased political visibility of sexuality as a component of human identity and increased (indeed, ubiquitous) representations of sexuality in mass media. In twenty-first-century global culture, sexuality is everywhere.

Sign

A sign is the basic unit within the signifying system. Ferdinand de Saussure defines a sign as the relation between a single signifier and signified, where a signifier is a sound image and a signified is a concept. We usually think of a sign, like a word, as being the connection between a sound and an object in the process of naming. The terms sign highlights the fact that a signifier/signified combination can take any form—spoken words, hand signals, raised dots, light flashes, and any other means of developing a code.

Signs within a structuralist linguistics analysis make meaning in two forms. The connection between a single signifier and a single signified is called "signification"; signification is always arbitrary, meaning that there is no organic or intrinsic connection between any particular signified and signifier. Signification as an arbitrary relation is what makes multiple meanings possible; the sound image "wrench" can have as its concept the metal plumbing tool or the act of tearing something away. The second way a sign can have meaning is called "value." An individual sign exists within a system of signs; you might think of the letters of the alphabet or the six positions in which a raised dot can be placed in Braille. A sign has value because it has meaning in relation to all the other signs in the system. The value of a sign consists in the fact that it is not any of the other signs in the system. The letter A in our alphabet has meaning because it is not the B, C, D, or E. A signifying system must contain at least two signs, each of which is different from the other so that you can tell them apart. Perhaps the simplest example of this is computer language, which consists of two positions of the switch: on and off. On is represented by 1 and off is represented by 0. The meaning or value of 1 is that it is not 0, and the value of 0 is that it is not one. A signifying system in which all the signs were the same would not make sense.

The ideas of signification and value also connect to the concepts langue and parole. An individual sign or parole has signification; it is the connection between a particular signifier and a particular signified which makes meaning. All the signs taken together constitute langue, and value is the meaning created by knowing that one sign is not any of the other signs in the system. When you look at signification, you look at an individual sign and take it apart to see what sound image is connected with what concept. When you look at value you look at langue as a whole and see how each sign is related to the system a whole.

Signification

The connection between a single signifier and a single signified is called "signification." Signification is always arbitrary, meaning that there is no organic or intrinsic connection between any particular signified and signifier. Signification as an arbitrary relation is what makes multiple meanings possible; the sound image "wrench" can have as its concept the metal plumbing tool or the act of tearing something away.

Signifyin'

This term is defined by Henry Louis Gates Jr. in his essay "The Blackness of Blackness: A Critique of the Sign and the Signifying Monkey" (1983). Gates plays with Saussure's idea of signification, which is the association of one signifier with one signified, to talk about a specifically African (and African American) use of language called "signifying" or "signifyin." Signifyin' in this context means playing a language game, usually of ritual insults, where one person tries to dominate another by coming up with the cleverest rhymes and rhythms. Rap, Hip-hop, and "yo' mama" jokes are all examples of such signifyin'. Gates notes that this form of verbal battle belongs to groups that are otherwise disempowered, and who use language in the absence of physical force. He traces the figure of the "signifyin' monkey" in two directions: to the racist stereotype of Africans and African Americans as monkeys or apes, and to African mythology and religious beliefs. In doing the latter he argues that literary theorists need to look beyond just the Western Greco-Roman traditions of rhetoric to explore other cultures' uses of language.

Simulacrum

In Latin, a simulacrum (plural simulacra) means a representation or image; in postmodern theory, the word is associated with Jean Baudrillard and the idea of cultures created via simulation or representation. Baudrillard's work traces the idea of simulacra through Western history, arguing that signs—or what we might call signifiers—became increasingly detached from reality (or signifieds); the first order of simulacra emerged in the Baroque period, when artifice and representation came to be valued over natural signs. With the advent of mass production, Baudrillard argues, following Walter Benjamin, the possibility of multiple copies destroyed the mystic aura of the original, creating a second-order simulacra where basic reality disappears. In the third order of simulacra, representations or signs have no relation to any reality whatsoever, but exist on their own terms and create their own reality; Baudrillard writes about Disneyland and Las Vegas as examples of third-order simulacra, where "reality" is always the constructed hyperreal. In Baudrillard's thought, one of the characteristics of postmodern culture is the pervasive "reality" of such third-order simulacra.

Specular image

The idea of the "specular," meaning the visible, is important in Lacanian psychoanalysis, particularly in the description of the mirror phase, where the baby first sees an image of itself as an integrated being by viewing its reflection in a mirror. The baby's first visual or specular experience of itself creates an illusion, an image, of the baby as whole and complete, a "self" like the caregivers around it. The baby then internalizes this specular image as its ego, its conception of its identity. Lacan calls this specular image a "misrecognition" because the baby does not have an integrated identity; rather, it is a set of fragmented and discontinuous parts. The experience of the specular image, however, provides the baby with a visual sense of wholeness that is affirmed when the baby enters the Symbolic Order and learns to express its ego identity with the signifiers "I" and "me."

Speech act

A term designating a verbal utterance that performs an action or makes something happen. When a minister or judge says, "I now pronounce you husband and wife," this statement changes the legal status of the two people being married. A speech act, also called an illocutionary act, can be a statement, command, question, or promise; it is a communication that follows certain rules and that assumes certain relations between the speaker and the listener. Speech acts are described in J. L. Austin's *How to Do Things with Words* (1962), and in the works of John R. Searle, including *Speech Acts: And Essay in the Philosophy of Language* (1969) and *Expression and Meaning: Essays in the Theory of Speech Acts* (1979).

Structuralism

Structuralism is a way of looking at the world that tries to reduce phenomena to their most basic level. Structuralism sees any phenomenon as consisting of two dimensions: units and rules. The model comes originally from Aristotelian science, and more specifically from Saussurean linguistics, and has been used in anthropology, mathematics, and literary and cultural studies among others; it was particularly influential in the era between World War II and the 1960s. Whatever its object of study, a structuralist analysis looks to find the most basic or fundamental parts of the system or structure, which are the *units* of that structure. Units combine with each other according to specific rules. Structuralism looks at the units and rules and how they work together to form any kind of structure, whether it is a signifying system, mathematical

equation, a building, or a cultural system like a kinship structure. Traditionally, structuralism takes a view of a phenomenon;
structuralists are not interested in changes over time or in history.
Structuralism in literary studies has focused primarily on classifying literary works according to the genre or narrative structure,
and is most useful for categorizing texts into particular groups
with similar characteristics rather than for analysing the content
of individual texts.

Subaltern

A term taken from the colonial military context meaning a non-
white soldier of inferior rank, which is used in postcolonial theory
to denote a member of the colonized population. Gayatri Spivak
uses the term specifically to refer to the lowest layers of a colonial
or postcolonial society: the homeless, the day laborers, the unem-
ployed, arguing that these subaltern populations are voiceless
and invisible in both colonial and post- or neocolonial cultures.
In her article "Can the Subaltern Speak?" (1988) Spivak focuses
on women as subalterns in debates between British and Indian
cultures around the issue of sati or widow-burning; women themselves do not participate, from either perspective, in the debate.

Subject

Perhaps no term is more ubiquitous in contemporary literary and cultural theory than "subject." In general, "subject" refers to what was
called the "self" in the humanist tradition: the concept of individual
identity or personhood. In post-structuralist thought, however, the
notion of selfhood or identity is subsumed under the idea that all
concepts of "self," like all experience and reality, are products of
language itself. The idea of "self" expressed in the word "I"—the
unique individual expression of experience—is in fact possible only
because the structure of language makes the word "I" possible. The
term "subject" encapsulates this idea, referring to the grammatical
structure of the subject (as in the subject of the sentence) that makes
possible the position of the human subject—the signified that the signifier "I" supposedly points to. The humanist "self" is described as

autonomous and creative; the post-structuralist "subject" is the creation of a structural position. "Subject" also encapsulates the idea that any individual is a product of systems and must follow the rules of those systems; a speaking subject is subjected to the rules of grammar, which one must follow if one is to be understood. The term "subject" thus conveys the idea of a position or space that is inhabited, in contrast to the humanist idea of the self that exists in an unchanging essential form; a subject is created by whatever context or structure posits a subject position, and is subjected to the rules of that system. A subject position within a structure makes possible the notion of the subject. You might think here of an auditorium with fixed seats as the system or structure; each seat is a subject position, which remains constant regardless of who sits in it. When you occupy a seat, you then see the world (the stage) from that position—your perspective is fixed, determined by your subject position regardless of any concept of individual identity or experience. This idea is particularly useful in literary studies, as all texts create subject positions from which acts of reading or interpretation occur.

Superego

The superego is one of three areas of the human psyche as mapped by Freud; the other two are the ego and the unconscious. The superego is equivalent to the conscience or moral sensibility, an internal voice that tells us what is right or wrong, and that creates emotions of fear and guilt for transgressions. In Freud's account, the superego is formed as a result of the resolution of the castration complex. A boy, desiring his mother and wanting to kill his father, sees a girl for the first time and believes she has had her penis cut off for a similar desire; fearing castration (which Freud defines as the removal of the penis), the boy represses his desires for his mother into the unconscious and creates the superego, which houses the punitive voice of his father as lawgiver. Freud's account of the female version of this is more ambiguous. The girl, having already been castrated, in Freud's formulation, has nothing to lose, and therefore no powerful psychic motive to create a superego that will judge her and keep her from wrongdoing. Because of this, Freud concluded, women have weaker superegos than men and are thus less capable of consistent moral judgment.

Symbolic

The third phase, following the Real and the Imaginary, in Lacanian psychoanalysis is the Symbolic Realm or Symbolic Order. It is the arena in which symbolic exchange happens. Entry into the Symbolic Realm marks the transition of the primitive infant into a civilized adult human who can represent itself and its world through symbols, specifically through the combination of signifiers and signifieds that create stable signs. Lacan's conception of the Symbolic draws on Freud's idea of the resolutions of the Oedipus and Castration Complexes as the movement from primitive being to civilized adult, from "nature" to "culture." It also borrows from Claude Levi-Strauss' anthropological theories on the idea of symbolic exchange as a fundamental structuring principle of all cultures, and from Ferdinand de Saussure the idea of linguistic representations, or signs, as the medium for this exchange.

A child enters into the Symbolic Realm after the mirror stage, in which it has internalized an image of itself as a whole being; the transition from the Imaginary into the Symbolic (a transition that is always incomplete) is marked by the child's ability to name that image of itself, its ego-ideal, as "me" or "I." Putting a linguistic signifier—the sound-image "I"—together with the concept of "self" as an integrated bounded whole completes the sign that, in language, means "selfhood." With the ability for self-representation, the ability to name one's own being and "I"dentity, the child becomes a language-using subject and can participate in symbolic or representational exchange. This participation requires that the language-using subject comes under the authority of the Phallus, which is the center of the Symbolic Realm. Unlike the humanist concept of the self as creating its own meaning, the subject within the Symbolic is subjected to the rules of language; meaning is a product not of the individual but of the structure of language and of culture itself. A person enters the Symbolic Order and takes up a subject position in relation to the Phallus; from this position a person can speak, use, and exchange signifiers, as long as the person acknowledges the power of the Phallus to control that exchange. The Phallus stands as the transcendental signified, the ultimate source of the meaning of the signifiers being exchanged; in relation to the Phallus, the subject is constituted as lack or absence, and feels constant (and unfulfillable) desire to occupy the central position of the Phallus.

Synchronic

Synchronic means any kind of analysis that does not take account of time. Structuralism usually relies on synchronic analysis; that is, it looks at a structure at a particular moment in time as if that structure had always existed and would always exist exactly the way it is at the moment of observation. Synchronic analyses are not interested in change or development or origin or endpoint; a synchronic analysis looks at something at a single moment in time. Diachronic analysis, by contrast, looks specifically for origins and changes as it examines a structure or phenomenon over a period of time. Structuralist analysis in linguistics anthropology and sociology are primarily synchronic forms of analysis; a structuralist analysis of the signifying system would be interested only in investigating what the structure is at a particular moment and not in determining how the system has changed or how it began.

Syntagmatic, syntagmatic relations

This term, also used by Saussure, refers to the way that signs within the signifying system make meaning through appearing in a certain order according to the rules of grammar for that signifying system. A syntagm is a grouping of words that makes some sort of sense and follows the structure of grammar. An example might be any phrase that makes sense: "when in the course of," "into thin air," "on top of," "you and I." A syntagmatic relationship is one where signs occur in sequence or parallel and work together to create meaning. The letters in a word have syntagmic relationship with one another as do the words in a sentence.

Theory

The dictionary defines "theory" as "the supposition or system of ideas explaining something." Theory, then, is explanation—coming up with ideas *why* something is the way it is. On another level, theory is a kind of meta-thinking: thinking about how you think about things. Theory exists in every discipline, in every kind of knowledge, and perhaps in every thought humans have about themselves and their world. In literary studies, we talk about "literary theory" as a means of explaining what literature is, what it does, and how we think about it. The modes of thinking and writing called "literary theory" come not just from literary studies, however; literary theory uses ways of thinking that come from a wide variety of other disciplines, including history, anthropology, linguistics, psychology, and even mathematics. In literature departments in universities, these ways of thinking are called "literary theory;" in other departments, they may be called something else, like "cultural theory" or "critical theory." The names suggest the fundamental interdisciplinarity of "theory" in the humanities and social sciences. What they all have in common is the study of human cultural texts: the forms of meaning humans produce, whether in literary form or in historical event, cultural ritual, or language. Cultural and literary theories study how humans use symbol systems to make meaning in and of their world and their experiences.

Which is not to say that all "theory" is the same in every discipline or department. Literary theory, the special province of literary studies, investigates the phenomena we call "literature," asking questions like what makes a "literary" text different from any other text—how is a novel different from a plumbing manual? Cultural theory has perhaps a wider scope, asking questions about how human cultures are organized and expressed; literary theory would in this sense be a subset of cultural theory. Literary theory is also referred to as "critical theory," usually in pointing to the post-structuralist forms of hermeneutics, deconstruction, reception theory, semiotics, and narratology, which dominated literary theory beginning in the late 1960s.

Critical theory, however, has a more precise and historically specific definition. Critical theory refers to the writings and philosophies emerging from the Frankfurt Institute of Social Research, established in 1923 in Frankfurt, Germany, to pursue studies in the humanities and social sciences that were independent of any public or private funding. "The Frankfurt School," as it became known, under the direction of Max Horkheimer, sponsored research in literary and aesthetic areas by thinkers such as Theodore Adorno, Leo Lowenthal, and Herbert Marcuse; the writings of Bertolt Brecht, Georg Lukacs, and Walter Benjamin were also associated with the Frankfurt School. Critical theory draws heavily on the works of Marx and Freud in investigating the operations of ideology; its goal was to find ways of understanding human culture that would help liberate people from the illusions of ideologies that distort or deny their objective interests. In this sense, critical theory has more to do with Marxist sociological and political theory than with literary theory per se; its focus on ideology, however, led many members of the Frankfurt School to investigate the role literary texts play in creating and maintaining ideologies. Walter Benjamin, for example, argued that art and literature are not just reflections of social relations but are among the many modes of production of social relations, as mediated by aesthetic (in contrast to economic) practices. The Frankfurt School closed in 1973 with the death of Max Horkheimer; Jürgen Habermas remains its most significant contemporary spokesperson.

Transnationalism

Transnationalism means something that transcends nationalism, something that is not limited by national boundaries or the concepts of what constitutes a "nation." In the twenty-first century, the global economy and the boundlessness of the internet help to loosen national divisions and create greater interconnectedness between people regardless of what country they belong to. Transnationalism in postcolonial theory refers to the situation of migratory or nonresident workers, who may be citizens of one country while living and working in another, and to the situation of people displaced, by war, disaster, or political upheaval, who may not have claim to any "home" country. Transnationalism also describes nongovernmental organizations (NGOs) in which people from a variety of countries work together to aid others; *Médecins sans Frontiéres* and *Greenpeace* are examples of transnational NGOs.

Unconscious

The unconscious is one of three areas of the human psyche mapped by Freud; the other two are the ego and the superego. The unconscious is perhaps the greatest "discovery" made by Freudian psychoanalysis: the idea that there is a part of our mind that is inaccessible to our conscious, rational mind and that governs our actions and thoughts in ways we cannot control or predict shattered the Cartesian model of the "self" who was capable of self-knowledge. Emerging at the end of the nineteenth century, the idea of a shadow self or hidden self appeared in a variety of forms, including Robert Louis Stevenson's *Dr. Jekyll and Mr. Hyde* (1886) which presents this hidden self as an uncontrollable bloodthirsty monster of sex and violence. Freud's unconscious is similarly the place where primitive lusts reside. Freud posited that the unconscious is formed through the correct resolution of the Oedipus and Castration Complexes, where the child who has wanted to have sex with its mother and to kill its father represses those incestuous forbidden desires. From that moment on, any thoughts or wishes that are unacceptable to the ego and the superego—to the conscious mind and to the conscience or moral sensibility—are repressed into the unconscious. The unconscious thus exists as a kind of prison for libidinal drives that threaten social order and civilization. The unconscious follows only the rule of the pleasure principle and does not recognize any "higher" authority or external reality.

By definition, what resides in the unconscious is inaccessible to the conscious mind through any direct route; you cannot think about what is unconscious. Freud maps out several ways that our conscious minds can get clues about the contents of the unconscious, however. First among these is dreams, which Freud argues are fantasies that fulfill wishes repressed into the unconscious; other routes include parapraxes or "Freudian slips," verbal mistakes (like typographical errors) that reveal unconscious contents and jokes. In all of these, material from the unconscious appears in coded or disguised form so that the conscious mind cannot know directly what the unconscious is saying. Through mechanisms such as condensation and displacement, the unconscious encodes its messages in forms that, like dreams or stories, need to be analysed and interpreted. Freud, and many psychoanalysts after him, posited that the creation of art and literature, as well as myth, appeared as expressions of the unconscious.

Freud argued that an enormous amount of psychic energy is expended in guarding the gates of the unconscious to keep the contents repressed; he associated that use of energy with neurosis, which as a medical doctor he hoped to cure. His method for this involved bringing the contents of the unconscious into consciousness through talking. The goal of Freudian psychoanalytic therapy

was to reduce the need for repression by having the ego or conscious mind look at and accept the libidinal drives contained in the
unconscious. *Wo es war, soll ich werden*: where it was, shall I be.
In this phrase Freud voiced his hope that the ego, the *ich*, would
take the place of the unconscious, the id *(das es)*. The idea that
talking about and interpreting the symbols that escape from the
unconscious can lead to the growth of a healthier ego underlies
most forms of psychotherapy since Freud.

For some psychoanalysts, however, Freud's goal of bringing the
contents of the unconscious into the consciousness is impossible.
In Lacan's formulation, the unconscious is the ground of being, the
original form of the mind; it is the consciousness that is created by
the unconscious, not the other way around. Lacan posits that our
primary psychic state is that of an ungoverned and ungovernable
unconscious, which consists of multiple chains of signifiers that
are constantly shifting and sliding; within this linguistic unconscious, no stable meaning—no words—is possible. Freud's rampant
libidinal drives in Lacan's version become shifting signifiers, which
constantly slide around each other, making any kind of definitive
meaning impossible because of différance . With no way to connect
a signifier to a signified, concepts like "I" have no meaning; there can
be no ego, no self, no "I"dentity within this Lacanian unconscious.
The conscious mind, the self that says "I," is an illusion created by
the unconscious, according to Lacan, during the mirror stage.

The conscious mind thus corresponds with the Symbolic Order,
with the structuring principle of the Phallus, the transcendental
signified, which stops the sliding chains of signifiers and holds
them in place so that one signifier can be associated with a single
definitive signified and words can have meaning. The unconscious,
however, is always capable of disrupting this order and decenter-
ing the Phallus. Insofar as Freud insisted that women, who have
already been castrated, have no powerful impetus for repressing
primitive libidinal desires, feminist theorists have posited that the
female unconscious is less well guarded than the male unconscious;
the female unconscious thus threatens the stability of the phallocentric Symbolic Order. Hélène Cixous names this feminine language, or l'ecriture feminine, as a means of using language that
does not follow the rules, that does not acknowledge the authority of the Phallus, and that speaks the uncontrollable unconscious
directly.

Value

Value is a term used by Ferdinand de Saussure referring to a structuralist view of language as a signifying system. Value and signification are the two ways in which signifying systems create meaning. A sign has "value" because it is not any other sign in the system; the value of a sign can only be known within the context of the whole system or langue. Signification, by contrast, is the arbitrary connection between a single signifier and a single signified to make an individual sign or parole. In this sense signification is a positive relation, and value is a negative relation.

The term value also has a variety of meanings in different theoretical contexts. In Marxism, for example, value describes kinds of work and exchange practices. An article has use value when you can use it; it has exchange value when you can trade it for something of equivalent worth. Workers create surplus value when they transform raw materials into finished goods, which is then appropriated by the owner of the means of production.

Major Figures

Adorno, Theodore

Theodore Adorno (1903–69), associated with the Frankfurt School, was a pioneering Marxist theorist of mass media and popular culture. Major works translated into English include *Prisms* (1967), *Negative Dialectics* (1973), *Notes to Literature*, Volumes One and Two (1991, 1992), *The Culture Industry: Selected Essays on Mass Culture* (1991), *Critical Models: Interventions and Catchwords* (1998), and *Dialectic of Enlightenment: Philosophical Fragments* (2002).

Althusser, Louis

Algerian-born French Marxist philosopher (1918–90) who is particularly associated with structuralist Marxism. He was first influenced by communist and Marxist politics in Europe after World War II; the disappearance of Stalin's doctrines from the Soviet Union in the 1950s and the student upheavals in Paris in May 1968 also heightened his allegiance to Marxism.

Althusser's writings concern rereading Karl Marx's works in order to fit them in with contemporary thought in the post-1968 European world; this meant rereading Marx to find his structuralist and post-structuralist elements. In *Reading 'Capital'* and *For Marx*, which he co-authored with Etienne Balibar, Althusser argued that Marx's works should be divided into two eras or phases: Marx's early texts were based on classical political economy and German philosophy whereas his works after 1845 develop new ways of thinking about politics and economics. Althusser claimed the later Marx as more truly "Marxist," reading works such as *The German Ideology* from an anti-humanist perspective.

Althusser is most known for his writings on Ideology, which draw on Marx's concept of the base/superstructure model and on Antonio Gramsci's ideas about hegemony. In his essay "Contradiction and Overdetermination," Althusser draws on psychoanalytic theory to introduce the concept of multiple causality to Marxist theory, arguing that the base/superstructure model is too linear to explain the complexities of ideological belief systems. Althusser liked Lacan's model of the structure of the unconscious and of language, and posited that Ideology functions along the same lines; he is among the first Marxists to work to meld Marxist and psychoanalytic theories.

Althusser argued that ideology is not merely a mimetic representation of the economic conditions of a society; rather, the realm of ideology is relatively autonomous of the economic base and has its own structures and modes of functioning. In "Ideology and Ideological State Apparatuses," Althusser discussed the mode by which Ideology interpellates subjects; in doing so he insists that belief systems and material practices are inseparable.

Althusser's writings had a major influence on many other post-structural theorists, including most notably Jacques Derrida, Slavoj Žižek, and Judith Butler. Major works translated into English include *Reading 'Capital'* and *For Marx* (with Etienne Balibar, 1970), *Lenin and Philosophy and Other Essays* (1971), and *Philosophy and the Spontaneous Philosophy of the Scientists and Other Essays* (1990).

Anzaldúa, Gloria

Anzaldúa (1942–2004) is a lesbian-feminist Chicana poet and cultural theorist. Major works include *This Bridge Called My Back: Writings by Radical Women of Color* (1981), *Borderlands/La Frontera: The New Mestiza* (1987), *Making Face, Making Soul/ Haciendo Caras: Creative and Critical Perspectives by Feminists of Color* (1990), and *This Bridge We Call Home: Radical Visions for Transformation* (2002).

Aristotle

Aristotle (384–322 BCE) is one of the founding fathers of Western philosophy. Though most of his works have disappeared in their original form, we have notes and fragments of his writings; modern versions of Aristotle's writings come from texts discovered or translated in the medieval period. Aristotle wrote about everything from science to morality; he is considered the father of logic, systematic reasoning, classification, and disciplinarity. His views on aesthetics, poetics, and rhetoric are most influential in literary and cultural theories.

Plato, Aristotle's teacher, had argued that all art was mimetic, that it was a copy of something that existed, and that whatever existed was itself merely a copy of the eternal form or Ideal version of that thing; art was thus doubly false, a copy of a copy, and therefore removed one from the Ideal. Art was dangerous also, according to Plato, because it addresses the emotional faculties rather than the intellectual ones, and thus is not subject to rational thought. For Aristotle, however, mimesis did not mean imitation but rather representation: art made its own representation of the world, which was not merely a copy of the real or the Ideal. Aristotle further disagreed with Plato in insisting that representation was a fundamental human intellectual trait, a form of knowing that could present universal intellectual, moral, and emotional truths. Aristotle outlines his ideas about representation and art in several works, most important of which is his Poetics, which discusses tragedy in detail; it is possible that the Poetics were originally two volumes, the second of which discussed comedy, but that volume is lost. In his analysis of the elements of tragedy, Aristotle lays out what would become the basic principles of literary analysis and literary theory throughout the Humanist tradition. He argued that the primary function of all representation, all art, was to present a complete and unified action with a clear beginning, middle, and end, all of which were linked by necessary and probable causation. The completeness, connectedness, and plausibility of the drama made it possible for audiences to identify with the characters and their moral flaws; this identification produced feelings of pity and fear in audience members and thus helped their moral growth.

Aristotle identifies these emotions of pity and fear felt by the audience as catharsis. Catharsis is variously defined as the purging of excess emotion, as the experience of extreme emotion in a controlled form, and as the cognitive process of learning from the emotional identification of characters undergoing trauma. These definitions argue that the audience's experience of drama is a source of pleasure and of knowledge, concepts fundamental to psychoanalytic theory and to literary theories derived from psychoanalysis.

Bakhtin, Mikhail M.

Russian philosopher, literary critic, and semiotician (1895–1975). He was active in debates about aesthetics and literature in the Soviet Union in the 1920s, but his works were suppressed by Trotsky and not known in the West until the 1960s. He is associated with the Russian formalist movement of the same period. He is best known for his discussions of the concepts of dialogism, heteroglossia, the chronotope, and the carnivalesque.

Bakhtin's main work, *The Dialogic Imagination*, contains four essays explaining these concepts. In the first essay, he discusses polyphony in the novels of Dostoevsky, noting that, while a character in a novel has an individual voice and speaks for a singular self, all the voices interact in a dialogue. The concept of the dialogic challenges the idea of a singular truth insisting that all social interaction consists of many voices interacting without the necessity for one voice to be "true" or "correct." In a dialogic interaction, the voice of one is heard by all and all voices influence all others, without a hierarchy of truth.

The concept of heteroglossia comes from Bakhtin's notion of the dialogic. Heteroglossia means "many languages"; Bakhtin notes that heteroglossia is another characteristic of novels, which flourish on the diversity of languages and characters. Poetry, by contrast, according to Bakhtin, is monologic and univocal; he is arguing here with the formalist method of reading, where one reads only the text without regard to any social context. Chronotope means, literally, "time space"; the creation of connected temporal and spatial relations is another characteristic of the "realism" created within the form of the novel.

Bakhtin's work on Rabelais examines the carnivalesque, the context in which all voices, regardless of class or status, interact and flourish together; he finds in Rabelais a grotesque realism that emphasizes the power of laughter to resist hierarchies and hypocrisy.

Bakhtin's major works translated into English include *Rabelais and His World* (1968), *The Dialogic Imagination: Four Essays*

(1981), *Problems of Dostoevsky's Poetics* (1984), *Speech Genres and Other Late Essays* (1986), and *Towards a Philosophy of the Act* (1993).

Barthes, Roland

Barthes (1915–80) was a French structuralist and post-structuralist cultural critic and theorist concerned with language, literature, and the social world. Notable works translated into English include *Mythologies* (1957), *Elements of Semiology* (1964), *S/Z* (1970), *Writing Degree Zero* (1972), *The Pleasure of the Text* (1973), and *Image/Music/Text* (1977).

Baudrillard, Jean

French sociologist and cultural theorist (1929–2007) associated with poststructuralism and postmodernism. A student of Pierre Bourdieu and Roland Barthes, he is part of the generation of French intellectuals and social activists who were influenced by the student protests in Paris in May 1968 along with Deleuze, Lyotard, Foucault, Derrida, and Lacan. He was particularly interested in semiotics, in the ways meanings are generated by sign systems, and in technologies of communication and mass culture.

Baudrillard's early works examined mass culture and marketing within capitalism, differing from classical Marxism by emphasizing the importance of consumption rather than production. Following Barthes, he argued that the concept of need is always socially constructed, that objects have meaning beyond their use value. Baudrillard named four ways that "value" operates within capitalism: objects have functional value because they do something; they have exchange value because they can be bought, sold, and traded; they have symbolic value for individual subjects; and they have sign value within a system of signs.

Baudrillard moved away from Marxism in the 1980s to explore theories of mass culture and mass media. His explorations pointed to the idea that there is no such thing as "reality" but rather only representations or simulations: a fundamental premise of postmodernism. Baudrillard argued that mass culture produced simulacra, versions of reality where meaning was prepackaged; this hyperreality replaces any possibility of a traditional "reality" in Western postmodern culture. The reproducibility of simulacra provides their primary form of value; Baudrillard uses the example of the atomic bomb, which is meant to be endlessly reproduced but never used. Baudrillard's influence can be seen in many types of popular culture, such as the movie *The Matrix*.

His major works in English include: *For a Critique of the Political Economy of the Sign* (1981), *Simulations* (1983), *America* (1988), *Cool Memories* (1990), *Fatal Strategies* (1990), *Symbolic Exchange and Death* (1993), *The Transparency of Evil* (1993), *The Illusion of the End* (1994), *Simulacra and Simulation* (1994), *The Gulf War Did Not Take Place* (1995), *Cool Memories II* (1996), *The Perfect Crime* (1996), *Fragments: Cool Memories III, 1990–1995* (1997), *The Vital Illusion* (2000), *Impossible Exchange* (2001), *Screened Out* (2002), and *The Spirit of Terrorism and Requiem for the Twin Towers* (2002).

Benjamin, Walter

German literary critic (1892–1940) associated with the Frankfurt School. Major works translated into English include *Illuminations* (1969) and *Reflections* (1978); his essays are collected in *The Work of Art in the Age of Its Technological Reproducibility, and Other Writings on Media* (2008).

Bhaba, Homi

Indian postcolonial theorist (1949–) interested in questions of hybridity and transnationality. Works include *Nations and Narration* (1990) and *The Location of Culture* (1994).

Bloom, Harold

American literary critic and theorist (1930–), professor at Yale, best known for his theory of the "anxiety of influence," which uses Freud's idea of Oedipal conflict to understand authorial intertextual relations. He was also part of the Yale Critics, theorists of deconstruction, along with Derrida and de Man. Major works include *The Anxiety of Influence: A Theory of Poetry* (1973), *A Map of Misreading* (1975), *Deconstruction and Criticism* (1980), *The Western Canon: The Books and School of the Ages* (1994), *How to Read and Why* (2000), *Where Shall Wisdom Be Found?* (2004), and *Anatomy of Influence: Literature as a Way of Life* (2011).

Brecht, Bertolt

German dramatist, director, founder of the Berliner Ensemble, poet, and theorist (1898–1956). Best known for his didactic epic theater, his dramatic works include *The Threepenny Opera* (1928), *Mother Courage and Her Children* (1941), and *The Caucasian Chalk Circle* (1945).

Brooks, Cleanth

American literary critic (1906–) associated with New Criticism. Major works include *The Language of Poetry* (1942), *The Well Wrought Urn* (1947), and, with W. K. Wimsatt, *Literary Criticism: A Short History* (1957).

Butler, Judith

American feminist philosopher and queer theorist (1956–). Major works include *Gender Trouble* (1990), *Bodies That Matter* (1993), *Excitable Speech* (1997), *The Psychic Life of Power: Theories in Subjection* (1997), *Contingency, Hegemony, Universality: Dialogues on the Left* (2000), *Precarious Life: The Powers of Mourning and Violence* (2004), *Undoing Gender* (2004), *Who Sings the Nation-State? Language, Politics, Belonging* (with Gayatri Spivak) (2007), and *Frames of War: When Is Life Grievable?* (2009).

Cixous, Hélène

Algerian-born French feminist philosopher, poet, dramatist, and novelist (1937–). Raised in a colonial context, she was active in the student riots in Paris in 1968, and was one of the founders of the University of Paris VIII at Vincennes in 1969; there she worked with Michel Foucault, Gerard Genette, Gilles Deleuze, Tzvetan Todorov, and Félix Guattari. In 1974 she established the Centre de Recherches en Etudes Féminines, the first women's studies program in Europe.

In the early 1970s, Cixous published several fictional texts in which she experimented with new forms of writing; in 1974 she published a collection of essays on Freud, Poe, and Joyce, exploring post-structural ideas of language, gender, and social change. Her most famous essay, "The Laugh of the Medusa," appeared in 1975. In it she describes a practice of "l'ecriture feminine," a mode of writing characterized by rupturing Western phallogocentric logic and representation; Cixous' writing style is itself an excellent example of "l'ecriture feminine."

In the next decade, Cixous devoted herself to the women's movement, helping to start a women's press, *Des Femmes*, and participating in the political group "Psychanalyse et Politique," or "Psych et Po." With Luce Irigaray and Julia Kristeva, Cixous is one of the mothers of post-structural feminist thought in Europe and the United States.

Her more recent work incorporates her political critiques into explorations of subjectivity, blurring lines between literature and critical essays with her radically fluid writing style.

Her major works translated into English include *To Live the Orange* (1979), *The Newly Born Woman* (1986), *Reading with Clarice Lispector* (1990), *The Book of Promethea* (1991), *Coming to Writing* (1991), *Manna: For the Mandelstams for the Mandelas* (1994), and *Hélène Cixous: Rootprints* (1997).

Deleuze, Gilles

French philosopher of postmodernism (1925–95). Deleuze's works fall into two categories: his essays on particular philosophers and artists, including Nietzsche, Foucault, and Kafka; and his writings on concepts, such as schizoanalysis and the body without organs. His works, which were bestsellers in France, were translated into English in the 1980s and 1990s, and became particularly influential in architecture, urban studies, film studies, musicology, gender studies, and literary theory.

Deleuze met Félix Guattari in Paris in May 1968, where both were involved in the student riots that helped create a new climate of intellectual and political action; in 1969, at the University of Paris VIII in Vincennes, they began working on *Anti-Oedipus: Capitalism and Schizophrenia*. *Anti-Oedipus* is a "deconstruction" of Marx and Freud, whom Deleuze and Guattari claim provided the two main modes of knowing in twentieth-century thought. They combine ideas of Marx and Freud in discussing "desiring-production" as a universal primary process, and argue that capitalism structures desiring-production via private property and the family. They use the model of schizophrenia as an example of desiring-production freed from these structures and unleashed; the schizophrenic is the transcendent unconscious embodied and uncontrolled.

In *A Thousand Plateaus*, the continuation of *Anti-Oedipus*, Deleuze and Guattari offer fourteen "chapters," which they define as planes or moments of intensity; one of these moments introduces the concept of the rhizome, a way of knowing that rejects Western logic and hierarchies. The model of Western philosophical thought, for Deleuze and Guattari, is that of a tree: its branches and leaves, all of its parts, can be traced back to a point of origin, a seed. They proffer instead the model of fungus, which has no beginning and no end, no central reference point; postmodern culture is rhizomatic rather than arboreal. The internet is an example of a rhizomatic structure: all sites are connected to all other sites and none are more important than the other.

Deleuze's major works translated into English include *Masochism: An Interpretation of Coldness and Cruelty* (1971), *Nietzsche and Philosophy* (1983), *Foucault* (1988), *Cinema I: The Movement-Image* (1986), *Cinema II: The Time-Image* (1989), *Difference and Repetition* (1994), *Negotiations* (1995), *Essays Critical and Clinical* (1997), and *Desert Island and Other Texts (1953–1974)* (2003). With Félix Guattari, he wrote *Anti-Oedipus* (1972), *A Thousand Plateaus* (1987), and *What Is Philosophy?* (1994).

de Man, Paul

Belgian-born literary critic (1919–83) associated with the Yale Critics, Jacques Derrida, and deconstruction. Major works include

Blindness and Insight: Essays in the Rhetoric of Contemporary Criticism (1971), *The Rhetoric of Romanticism* (1984), *The Resistence to Theory* (1986), and *Aesthetic Ideology* (1996).

Derrida, Jacques

Algerian-born philosopher (1930–2004) who developed deconstruction. His works have had an enormous influence on literary theory and continental philosophy. His experience growing up in a French colony and as a Jew during World War II shaped his adult interests in language and politics.

Derrida studied phenomenology at the *École Normale Supérieure* in Paris in the 1950s; his colleagues there included Gille Deleuze, Michel Foucault, Louis Althusser, Jean-François Lyotard, and Roland Barthes. In 1966 he attended a conference at Johns Hopkins University on "The Language of Criticism and the Sciences of Man," where he delivered "Structure, Sign, and Play in the Discourse of the Human Sciences," the lecture that introduced the fundamental ideas of deconstruction. In this essay, he uses Levi-Strauss' insistence that the human mind functions through creating categories of binary oppositions to critique Western philosophy's reliance on this hierarchical dualism, where one term of an opposition is valued over another term. Derrida suggests that these binaries are not forms of "truth" or universal structure, but rather constructions that depend for their stability on maintaining an absolute separation which can be ruptured.

In 1967 Derrida published three major works articulating his theories: *Writing and Difference*, *Speech and Phenomena*, and *Of Grammatology*, for the last of which Gayatri Spivak wrote an introduction and did the English translation. All three of these works address the idea of deconstruction though none of them define it; Derrida's writing style resists making logical arguments because such writing replicates the logocentrism of Western philosophy. Rather, his writings are evocative and read more like literary works than like scholarly arguments—a choice that has frustrated many of Derrida's readers.

Derrida taught at the *École Normale* until 1983, when he became the "Director of Studies" in "Philosophical Institutions" at the *École des Hautes Études en Sciences Sociales* in Paris. He was also a frequent visiting professor in the United States, teaching at the University of California at Irvine, Johns Hopkins, Yale, and the New School.

Derrida published more than 40 books during his lifetime. His major works translated into English include *Of Grammatology* (1974), *Writing and Difference* (1978), *Margins of Philosophy* (1982), *Glas* (1986), *The Postcard from Socrates to Freud and Beyond* (1987), *Dissemination* (1991), *Aporias* (1993), *Spectres of Marx* (1994), *Monolinguism of the Other* (1998), *The Work of Mourning* (2001), and *Without Alibi* (2002).

Eco, Umberto

Italian semiotician and novelist (1932–). Critical works in English include *A Theory of Semiotics* (1975), *The Role of the Reader: Explorations in the Semiotics of Texts* (1979), *Faith in Fakes: Travels in Hyper Reality* (1986), *The Limits of Interpretation* (1990), *Six Walks in the Fictional Woods* (1994), *Kant and the Platypus: Essays on Language and Cognition* (1999), *Mouse or Rat?: Translation as Negotiation* (2003), and *Turning Back the Clock: Hot Wars and Media Populism* (2007). Fiction in English includes *The Name of the Rose* (1980), *Foucault's Pendulum* (1988), *The Island of the Day Before* (1995), *Baudolino* (2000), *The Mysterious Flame of Queen Loana* (2005), and *The Prague Cemetery* (2010).

Eliot, T(homas) S(tearns)

American-born poet, playwright, and literary critic (1888–1965) who was awarded the Nobel Prize in Literature in 1948. Eliot's ideas about the autonomy of the poem laid the groundwork for New Criticism. Major critical works include "Tradition and the Individual Talent" (1919), *The Sacred Wood: Essays, Poetry, and Criticism* (1920), and *The Use of Poetry and the Use of Criticism* (1933). His poetic works are widely anthologized, and all of his writings are available in collected editions.

Fish, Stanley

American literary theorist (1938–) associated primarily with reader-response criticism and affective stylistics. Major works include *Surprised by Sin: The Reader in 'Paradise Lost'* (1967), *Is There a Text in This Class? The Authority of Interpretive Communities* (1980), *Doing What Comes Naturally: Change, Rhetoric, and the Practice of Theory in Literary and Legal Studies* (1989), *Professional Correctness: Literary Studies and Political Change* (1999), *Save the World on Your Own Time* (2008), and *How to Write a Sentence: And How to Read One* (2011).

Foucault, Michel

French philosopher and historian (1926–84) who invented new methodologies for critical studies of social institutions, including psychiatry, medicine, and the "human sciences." His explorations of institutional organization in the asylum, the clinic, the prison, and of the mechanisms controlling and creating the category "sexuality" have had a profound influence on contemporary social science and cultural studies.

Foucault began his career as a structuralist but came to reject all labels in favor of calling himself simply "Nietzschean." His work in the early 1960s shows the influence of structuralism, and by the mid-1960s Foucault's perspective shifted, along with that of Lacan and Roland Barthes, to post-structuralism. He was deeply affected by the events of May 1968 in Paris and became the first head of the philosophy department at the newly created University of Paris VIII at Vincennes in 1969. He was elected to the Collége de France as professor of the History of Systems of Thought, and served as a visiting professor at the University of California at Berkeley. He died of an AIDS-related illness while still working on his projected six-volume work on the history of sexuality. His major works in English include *Madness and Civilization* (1961), *The Birth of the Clinic* (1963), *The Order of Things* (1966), *The Archeology of Knowledge* (1969), *Discipline and Punish* (1975), and *The History of Sexuality: Volume I, The Will to Knowledge* (1976), Volume II, *The Use of Pleasure* (1984), and Volume III, *The Care of the Self* (1984).

Freud, Sigmund

Freud (1856–1939) was a Viennese medical doctor who was the founding father of psychoanalysis. Freud's ideas about the unconscious and human sexuality have had a profound influence on twentieth-century thought in countless directions, from literary criticism to postmodernism; virtually all forms of psychotherapy trace their roots to Freud's psychoanalysis.

Freud trained as a medical doctor and did his early research in anatomy and physiology. He became interested in the problem of hysteria, sets of physical symptoms with no discernible physiological cause, often associated with women's nervous constitution. Freud studied in Paris with J. M. Charcot, the leading expert on neurosis and hysteria, and learned from him the technique of hypnosis.

In Vienna, Freud worked with Wilhelm Fleiss and Josef Breuer to explain hysteria; he began to theorize that the root of all hysteria was some kind of sexual trauma, and eventually concluded that psychosomatic illnesses and neurotic disorders were the result of repressed sexual memories from early childhood. His subsequent theorizing, based on his observations from clinical practice, included the foundational concepts of the unconscious, infantile sexual desire, the Oedipus and Castration Complexes, penis envy, and the superego. Freud's final years were spent working to expand his clinical observations about individual patients into universal theories about the nature of art, religion, literature, and civilization in general, all of which he referred back to his formulations about the unconscious and the Oedipus Complex.

It is virtually impossible to describe thoroughly Freud's influence on twentieth-century thought; Freudian psychoanalysis is synonymous with modernism. Though many have questioned the scientific validity of Freud's theories, they have been accepted and celebrated in a host of disciplines and cultural forms, including and especially popular culture and literary theory. Lacan reworked Freud from a post-structuralist perspective, and post-structuralist feminist theory also rewrites Freud, seeing him as sexist, Eurocentric, phallogocentric, and heteronormative.

All of Freud's writings are available in English in *The Standard Edition of the Complete Works of Sigmund Freud* in 24 volumes, spanning 1953–72. His major works, listed chronologically, include

The Interpretation of Dreams (1900), *The Psychopathology of Everyday Life* (1901), *Jokes and Their Relation to the Unconscious* (1905), *Three Essays on the Theory of Sexuality* (1905), *Totem and Taboo* (1913), *Introductory Lectures on Psychoanalysis* (1916–17), *The Future of an Illusion* (1927), *Civilization and Its Discontents* (1930), *New Introductory Lectures on Psychoanalysis* (1933), and *Moses and Monotheism* (1939).

Gadamer, Hans-Georg

German philosopher (1900–2002) important in the development of hermeneutics along with Heidegger; his work influenced that of Jacques Derrida, Paul Ricoeur, and Jürgen Habermas. Major works translated into English include *Truth and Method* (1975), *Philosophical Hermeneutics* (1976), *Reason in the Age of Science* (1981), *Philosophical Apprenticeships* (1985), and *Literature and Philosophy in Dialogue: Essays in German Literary Theory* (1993).

Gates, Henry Louis Jr.

African American literary theorist, historian, and cultural critic (1950–). Major works include *Figures in Black: Words, Signs, and the "Racial" Self* (1987), *The Signifying Monkey* (1988), *Loose Canons: Notes on the Culture Wars* (1992), *Thirteen Ways of Looking at a Black Man* (1997), *The African American Century: How Black Americans Have Shaped Our Century* (2000), *Finding Oprah's Roots: Finding Your Own* (2007), and *Tradition and the Black Atlantic: Critical Theory in the African Diaspora* (2010).

Geertz, Clifford

American anthropologist (1926–); he pioneered the methodology of "thick description" in cultural studies. Major works include *The Interpretation of Cultures* (1973), *Local Knowledge: Further Essays in Interpretive Anthropology* (1983), and *Works and Lives: The Anthropologist as Author* (1988).

Genette, Gérard

French-born structuralist critic (1930–) associated with narratology and with semiotics. Major works translated into English include *Narrative Discourse: An Essay in Method* (1980), *Figures of Literary Discourse* (1982), *Narrative Discourse Revisited* (1988), *Mimologics* (1995), and *Paratexts: Thresholds of Interpretation* (1997).

Gilbert, Sandra and Gubar, Susan

Sandra Gilbert (1936–) and Susan Gubar (1944–) are American feminist literary critics and historians. Best known for their groundbreaking feminist reworking of Harold Bloom's "anxiety of influence," their works include *The Madwoman in the Attic* (1979), the three-volume *No Man's Land* (1987–88), their edition of the *Norton Anthology of Literature by Women: The Traditions in English* (1985, revised 1996), and *Masterpiece Theatre: An Academic Melodrama* (1995).

Greimas, A(lgirdas) J(ulien)

Greimas (1917–92) was a Russian-born semiotician, who was influenced by Levi-Strauss, Propp, and Saussure, and who helped expand semiotics into post-structuralist realms. Major works translated into English include *Semiotics and Language: An Analytical Dictionary* (with J. Courtés, 1982), *On Meaning: Selected Writings in Semiotic Theory* (1987), *The Social Sciences: A Semiotic View* (1989), and, with Jacques Fontanille, *The Semiotics of Passion: From States of Affairs to States of Feelings* (1993).

Guattari, Félix

French philosopher and psychoanalyst (1930–92). He had been a student of, and was analysed by, Jacques Lacan, and had a clinical practice at La Borde, an experimental psychiatric clinic where he studied schizophrenia and modern culture, and advocated analytic methods that broke with the Freudian traditions. Involved in the upheavals of May 1968 in Paris, he met Gilles Deleuze at the University of Paris VIII in Vincennes in 1969, and they began working on *Anti-Oedipus: Capitalism and Schizophrenia*, which was published in 1972. With Deleuze he also wrote *A Thousand Plateaus* (1980), the "sequel" to *Anti-Oedipus*, and *What Is Philosophy?* (1991). His major works also include *Molecular Revolution: Psychiatry and Politics* (1984), *The Three Ecologies* (1989), *Chaosmosis: An Ethico-Aesthetic Paradigm* (1992), *Soft Subversions* (1996), and *The Machinic Unconscious* (2011).

Habermas, Jürgen

German-born philosopher (1929–) associated with the Frankfurt School, who worked with Adorno, Horkheimer, Gadamer, and Ricoeur in developing philosophical hermeneutics. He is known particularly for his concepts of "communicative rationality" and the public sphere. Major works translated into English include *The Structural Transformation of the Public Sphere* (1962), *Toward a Rational Society* (1967), *Technology and Science as Ideology* (1968), *Knowledge and Human Interests* (1971), *Communication and the Evolution of Society* (1976), *The Theory of Communicative Action* (1981), *The Philosophical Discourse of Modernity* (1985), *Between Facts and Norms: Contributions to a Discourse Theory of Law and Democracy* (1992), *The Inclusion of the Other* (1996), *The Postnational Constellation* (1998), and *Between Naturalism and Religion: Philosophical Essays* (2008).

Hirsch, E(ric) D(onald)

Hirsch (1928–) is an American literary critic and theorist of hermeneutics, composition, and cultural literacy who taught at the University of Virginia. Major works include *Validity in Interpretation* (1967), *The Aims of Interpretation* (1976), *The Philosophy of Composition* (1981), *Cultural Literacy: What Every American Needs to Know* (1987), *The Dictionary of Cultural Literacy* (1988; revised 2002), and *The Making of Americans: Democracy and Our Schools* (2010).

Horkheimer, Max

Max Horkheimer (1895–1973) was a German and Jewish philosopher, and director of the Frankfurt Institute for Social Research. He was exiled from Germany during the Nazi regime; he continued to run the Institute in the United States, which he reopened in Frankfurt from 1949 until its closure in 1958. Major works translated into English include *Traditional and Critical Theory* (1937), *The Eclipse of Reason* (1947), and *The Dialectic of Enlightenment* with Theodor Adorno (1947).

Irigaray, Luce

Belgian-born lesbian and feminist psychoanalyst and philosopher (1932–). Best known for her critiques of gender, sexuality, and language in Freud and Lacan, her books translated into English include *This Sex Which Is Not One* (1977), *When Our Lips Speak Together* (1977), *And the One Doesn't Stir Without the Other* (1979), *Speculum of the Other Woman* (1985), *Elemental Passions* (1992), *An Ethics of Sexual Difference* (1993), *To Speak Is Never Neutral* (2002), and *Sharing the Word* (2008).

Iser, Wolfgang

German literary theorist and critic (1926–2007) associated with the Constance School of Reception Aesthetics and reader-response theory. Important works translated into English include *The Implied Reader* (1974), *Prospecting: From Reader Response to Literary Anthropology* (1989), *The Fictive and the Imaginary: Perspectives in Literary Anthropology* (1991), *The Range of Interpretation* (2000) and *How to Do Theory* (2006).

Jakobson, Roman

Russian semiotician and literary scholar (1896–1982) associated with Russian formalism and structuralism; his essay, co-written with Claude Levi-Strauss, on Baudelaire's "Les Chats" was highly influential in articulating the premises of structuralist analysis. Works translated into English include *Selected Writings 1971–1985*, in six volumes, *Six Lectures of Sound and Meaning* (1978), *The Framework of Language* (1980), and *Verbal Art, Verbal Sign, Verbal Time* (1985).

Jameson, Fredric

American Marxist literary and cultural critic (1934–) who places the ideas of of Adorno, Benjamin, and Marcuse in conversation with post-structuralist and postmodernist theories. Major works include *Marxism and Form: 20th Century Dialectical Theories of Literature* (1971), *The Prison-House of Language: A Critical Account of Structuralism and Russian Formalism* (1972), *The Political Unconscious: Narrative as a Socially Symbolic Act* (1981), *The Ideologies of Theory: Essays 1971–1986*, 2 volumes (1988), *Signatures of the Visible* (1990), *Postmodernism, or, the Cultural Logic of Late Capitalism* (1991), *The Cultural Turn: Selected Writings on the Postmodern, 1983–1998* (1998), *Jameson on Jameson: Conversations on Cultural Marxism* (2007), and *Representing Capital: A Reading of Volume One* (2011).

Kristeva, Julia

Bulgarian-born psychoanalytic feminist theorist (1941–) who trained with Jacques Lacan; her works synthesize elements of Marxist and psychoanalytic theories in exploring relations between language and the self. Major works translated into English include *Desire in Language: A Semiotic Approach to Literature and Art* (1980), *Powers of Horror: An Essay on Abjection* (1982), *The Revolution in Poetic Language* (1984), *Tales of Love* (1987), *Black Sun: Depression and Melancholy* (1989), *Nations Without Nationalism* (1993), *Hannah Arendt: Life Is a Narrative* (2001), and *Hatred and Forgiveness* (2010).

Lacan, Jacques

French psychoanalyst (1901–81) who expanded on Freud to build post-structuralist theories of human identity, language, gender, and philosophy. Lacan made psychoanalysis central to the study of the "human sciences," from anthropology to literary criticism.

Lacan's original training was in medicine and psychiatry; his interest in psychosis led to his association with surrealists Georges Bataille, Salvador Dali, and Pablo Picasso, and his interest in surrealist language experimentation.

Lacan pioneered ideas of a non-ego based psychoanalysis in his paper on the Mirror Phase in 1936; his later works elaborated on the idea that the ego was an illusion, an imaginary construct created by the unconscious to guard against the knowledge of the fragmented body and self. Lacan argued that identity was always the product of a dialectic with an Other, and that the unified singular ego was a mask disguising a fragmented subjectivity.

Lacan called for psychoanalysis to return to Freud, much like his friend Althusser's call to return to Marx; Lacan wanted to reread Freud in light of structuralist views of language use, drawing on Saussure, Jakobson, and Levi-Strauss. Combining Freud's idea of the Oedipus Complex as a cultural universal with Levi-Strauss' universal structures of myth as language, Lacan articulated the idea of the unconscious as structured like a language.

Lacan reformulated the resolution of the Oedipus Complex as the entry into the Symbolic Order, which enabled a subject to use representational language, particularly the signifier "I" to denote the concept of "self."

Lacan's ideas have had enormous influence on a number of post-structural literary and cultural theorists, including Hélène Cixous, Luce Irigaray, Gilles Deleuze and Felix Guattari, Jacques Derrida, Jane Gallop, and Slavoj Žižek.

Lacan taught a weekly seminar at the *École Freudienne de Paris* from 1963 to 1980; his published works are largely transcripts of these seminars and of Lacan's papers. Not all have been translated into English. His major works in English include *Écrits: A Selection* (1977), *The Seminar of Jacques Lacan*, Book I (1988), Book II (1998), and Book III (2000), and *The Four Fundamental Concepts of Psychoanalysis* (1994).

Leavis, F(rank) R(aymond)

British literary critic and teacher (1895–1978) who, with his wife Queenie, was a central figure in Cambridge criticism: a philosophy of literary interpretation aligned with New Criticism in emphasizing close reading and intellectual rigor. Major works include *New Bearings in English Poetry* (1932), *The Great Tradition* (1948), and *The Living Principle: "English" as a Discipline of Thought* (1975).

Levi-Strauss, Claude

Belgian-born French anthropologist and cultural theorist (1908–2009); he is one of the founding fathers of structuralism. Levi-Strauss argued that there were universal structures of the human mind and culture, and that these universals were apparent in myth, ritual, and symbolic action.

Levi-Strauss and his wife Dina did field work in Brazil in the 1930s and lived in Paris until 1941, when Levi-Strauss, being of Jewish descent, emigrated to the United States. With Roman Jakobson, he was part of a group of French academics-in-exile who used Saussurean structural linguistics to develop structuralism in the human sciences; he also worked with anthropologist Franz Boas at Columbia University. He returned to Paris in 1948 and published his dissertation on *The Elementary Structures of Kinship*, arguing that social organization can be explained by looking not at specific family formations but at the structural relationships all families share.

Levi-Strauss gained international fame for his memoir about his fieldwork, *Tristes Tropiques*, in 1955; his writings in the late 1950s and early 1960s combined structural anthropology with philosophical explorations of the universal or structural qualities of the human mind. In *Le Pensée Sauvage* (badly translated into English as *The Savage Mind*) he laid out a theory of mind, culture, and politics that presented an argument with Sartrean existentialism.

Levi-Strauss' contributions to twentieth-century thought include his emphasis on structure in analysing kinship and social relations, his emphasis on binary oppositions as a fundamental structure of the human mind, his identification of myth as a form of language, and his analysis of culture as symbolic communication. His thinking influenced many post-structuralist theorists, including Derrida, Bourdieu, and Lacan; his writings introduced the concepts of bricoleur, engineer, and binary opposition.

His major works in English include *The Savage Mind* (1962), *Structural Anthropology* (1963), *The Elementary Structures of Kinship* (1969), *The Raw and the Cooked* (1970), *From Honey to Ashes* (1973), *Tristes Tropiques* (1973), *The Naked Man* (1981), *Way of the Masks* (1988), and *The Origin of Table Manners* (1990).

Lukács, Georg

Hungarian-born literary and political theorist (1885–1971) who was a major figure in the Western Marxist critique of aesthetics and ideology. His major works translated into English include *The Historical Novel* (1962), *History and Class Consciousness: Studies in Marxist Dialectics* (1971), and *Theory of the Novel* (1971).

Lyotard, Jean-François

French literary critic and philosopher of phenomenology and the sublime (1924–98); he is most well known for his articulation of the idea of the postmodern. From 1969 to 1987 he taught at the University of Paris VIII at Vincennes, which had been founded in 1969 as a direct result of the student protests of 1968; his fellow faculty there included Michel Foucault, Gilles Deleuze, Felix Guattari, and Hélène Cixous. He also served as professor of Critical Theory at the University of California at Irvine, and as a visiting professor at Johns Hopkins University, University of California at Berkeley, Yale, Emory, and University of California San Diego.

Lyotard was among the first theorists of postmodernism, which arose from his critique of the Enlightenment endeavor to find human universals, things that all cultures and all peoples had in common. Such universals depended on what Lyotard called "metanarratives" or "grand narratives" that constitute the basic premises of a mode of knowing; the metanarrative of science, for example, is the idea that everything in the world is knowable through observation and deduction. Marxism, psychoanalysis, and logic are among Lyotard's targets, examples of theories that rely on grand narratives.

Postmodernism, for Lyotard, is not a specific time period or historical movement so much as a way of organizing knowledge; he argues that postindustrial Western society no longer manufactures physical goods but rather makes forms of knowledge. Knowledge in this sense is no longer the Enlightenment search for "truth," but the result of a process of discursive construction and commodification.

Lyotard's postmodernism is characterized by the mistrust of metanarratives in favor of micronarratives—modes of thinking and knowing that explain local or temporary phenomena rather than striving to find "universal truth." He draws on Ludwig Wittgenstein's model of language games to acknowledge the multiplicity of interpretive frameworks and communities of meaning at work in postmodern culture, much as Mikhail Bakhtin does in his definition of heteroglossia. An example of this kind of multiplicity might be two people who speak different languages; to "translate" one language into another, or both into a third, privileges one language, thus one culture, one mode of knowing, over another. Lyotard argues that postmodern knowledge consists of ideas bound by geography and time period, and stories that are discontinuous, fragmentary, and incomplete, which explain local or temporary phenomena without trying to build a universal theory.

When such grand narratives disappear or are discredited, according to Lyotard, what is left are flows of desire, temporary alliances, and strategic identifications that do not make claim to be always true, essential, or unchanging. Lyotard's postmodern emphasizes disruption and discontinuity; history is not a continuous story but multiple microstories about moments that disrupt or undermine existing assumptions and power structures, such as the riots in Paris of 1968.

Lyotard's ideas are influential for all postmodern theories, especially those of Deleuze and Guattari. His major works in English include *The Postmodern Condition: A Report on Knowledge* (1984), *Just Gaming* (1985), *The Differend: Phrases in Dispute* (1989), *Libidinal Economy* (1993), *Lessons on the Analytic of the Sublime* (1994), *Toward the Postmodern* (1998), and *Postmodern Fables* (1999).

Macherey, Pierre

French-born Marxist literary theorist influenced by Louis Althusser (1938–), who examined the ideologies underlying major trends in twentieth-century literary criticism. Major works translated into English include *Reading Capital* with Louis Althusser, Étienne Balibar and Jacques Ranciére (1965), *A Theory of Literary Production* (1978), *The Object of Literature* (1995), and *In a Materialist Way: Selected Essays* (1998).

Marcuse, Herbert

German American Marxist philosopher (1898–1979) and member of the Frankfurt School who remained in the United States after World War II and whose writings influenced the American New Left in the 1960s, especially regarding sexual liberation. Major works in English include *Eros and Civilization: A Philosophical Inquiry into Freud* (1955), *One-Dimensional Man* (1964), *Negations: Essays in Critical Theory* (1968), *An Essay on Liberation* (1969), *Counterrevolution and Revolt* (1972), and *The Aesthetic Dimension: Toward a Critique of Marxist Aesthetics* (1978).

Marx, Karl

German economist, historian, philosopher, and revolutionary (1818–83). He was the founder of the theory of Marxism, perhaps the most profoundly influential political and economic theory and practice shaping the twentieth-century world; his writings inspired the creation of nations following Marxist and communist principles, including the Soviet Union and China.

Marx's ideas were a fundamental critique of the organizing structure, and resultant inequality, of the capitalist economic system. His critique of capitalism came in part from the political economic theories of Adam Smith and David Ricardo; his philosophy of history, which is called historical or dialectical materialism, evolved from Marx's reading of Hegel. He was also influenced by the writings of J. J. Rousseau and Charles Fourier on socialism and by Frederich

Engels' analysis of the British working class. Marx combined these elements to create a theory explaining how history and economics worked—and, just as importantly, how to change them.

Marx reversed Hegel and idealist philosophy, arguing that human consciousness is the product of material culture and social relations, not the other way around. Marx's historical materialism posited that all social conditions, practices, and beliefs come from the economic or material organization of a culture; cultural change is thus a product of changes in material practice and action.

Marx was caught up in the European social upheavals of the 1840s, including the movements for socialism, communism, and English Chartism, all of which were political and philosophical responses to monarchical government and the growth of working-class poverty, the result of burgeoning capitalism. He expressed his revolutionary ideas in print in various radical newspapers that the Prussian government tried to suppress, causing Marx to move to Cologne, Paris, and Brussels in search of freedom of speech.

The year 1848 in Europe saw rebellions, protests, and revolts against monarchies as well as the publication of *The Communist Manifesto*, written by Marx and Engels. The *Manifesto* laid out two basic principles of Marxism. First, the idea that history is the history of class struggle, which, as the feudal power of monarchy gave way to the capitalist system, pitted the proletariat, or working classes, against the bourgeoisie, or owners of the means of production; and second, that communism would reveal the contradictions and exploitations inherent in the capitalist system and thus proceed to overthrow it. The radical ideas contained in *The Communist Manifesto* caused Marx to be expelled from Europe; he moved to London in 1849, where he lived until his death in 1883.

Marx published the first volume of *Capital* in 1867, a lengthy analysis of the capitalist mode of production, which contained his theory of surplus value and the explanation of the exploitation of workers by owners. He hoped to see Russia overthrow its monarchy and move directly into communism, bypassing the capitalist phase of development, but did not live to see the Russian Revolution or the development of communist nations.

Several of Marx's concepts are explained in *Key Terms*, including alienation, base/superstructure, capitalism, ideology, Marxism, and value.

Nietzsche, Friedrich

German philosopher (1844–1900) whose writings marked an epistemic shift away from humanist assumptions; his works are often cited as fundamental to post-structuralist philosophy and theory. His discussions of "das Id" influenced Freud's concepts of the ego and the unconscious, and his use of the rhetorical strategy of metalepsis or inversion appears in deconstruction. All of his works are available in English translation; convenient collections and anthologies include *The Portable Nietzsche* (1954) and *Basic Writings of Nietzsche* (1966). Many theorists have written specifically about Nietzsche's influence, including Gilles Deleuze, Jacques Derrida, Hans-Georg Gadamer, Martin Heidegger, and Luce Irigaray.

Propp, Vladimir

Russian formalist critic (1895–1970), best known for his study of the basic principles of folktales, a project that influenced the development of structuralism and narratology in the 1960s. His major work translated into English is *Morphology of the Folktale* (1958).

Ransom, John Crowe

American literary critic and poet (1888–1974) associated with New Criticism, who argued that literary criticism needed to become more scientific or systematic. Major critical works include *The New Criticism* (1941) and *Beating the Bushes: Selected Essays, 1941–1970* (1997).

Richards, I(vor) A(rmstrong)

British literary critic (1893–1979) associated with New Criticism that he called "practical criticism" the practice of close reading. Major works include *The Principles of Literary Criticism* (1925), *Science and Poetry* (1926), *Coleridge on Imagination* (1929), *Practical Criticism* (1929), and *Speculative Instruments* (1955).

Ricoeur, Paul

French philosopher (1913–2005) combining hermeneutics and phenomenology, aligned with Heidegger and Gadamer, who taught at the Sorbonne, where Jacques Derrida was his assistant, and the University of Chicago. Major works in English include *Freedom and Nature* (1965), *The Symbolism of Evil* (1967), *Freud and Philosophy: An Essay on Interpretation* (1970), *The Conflict of Interpretations: Essays in Hermeneutics* (1974), *The Rule of Metaphor: Multi-Disciplinary Studies in the Creation of Meaning in Language* (1978), *Hermeneutics and the Human Sciences: Essays on Language, Action, and Interpretation* (1981), *Time and Narrative*, three volumes (1983–85), *From Text to Action: Essays in Hermeneutics II* (1991), *The Just* (2000), and *Living Up to Death* (2009).

Said, Edward

Palestinian-born American literary and cultural critic (1935–2003), who was considered one of the founders of postcolonial studies and a major figure in postcolonial theory. He was a professor of English and Comparative Literature at Columbia University. His major work, *Orientalism*, draws on Foucault and Derrida in presenting a post-structuralist understanding of how imperialism operates via discursive practices. He was also an outspoken advocate for Palestinian state rights.

His major works include *Joseph Conrad and the Fiction of Autobiography* (1966), *Beginnings: Intention and Method* (1975), *Orientalism* (1978), *The Question of Palestine* (1979), *Covering Islam: How the Media and the Experts Determine How We See the Rest of the World* (1981), *The World, the Text, and the Critic* (1983), *Nationalism, Colonialism, and Literature* (1990), *Culture and Imperialism* (1993), *The Politics of Dispossession* (1994), and *Representations of the Intellectual* (1994).

Saussure, Ferdinand de

Saussure (1857–1913) was a Swiss linguist and one of the founders of twentieth-century semiotics whose work paved the way for the development of structuralism. Saussure taught at the University of Geneva, where in 1907 he offered the first of three versions of his Course in General Linguistics, his most famous work. Saussure never wrote the Course as a book; rather, when it was published in 1916, after his death; it was based on the class notes taken by his students.

Saussure's primary idea was that language has to be analysed and understood as a system, not as a bundle of actual word usages. This way of looking at language laid the groundwork for the development of structuralist linguistics. He also articulated the concept of the sign as an arbitrary relation between a signifier and a signified. These ideas about sign and structure powerfully influenced the thinking of structuralist theorists such as Roland Barthes, Claude Levi-Strauss, and Jacques Lacan.

Saussure's *Course in General Linguistics* was published in English in 1974.

Spivak, Gayatri

Indian-born cultural theorist (1942–), a founder of the field of postcolonial studies who describes herself as "a practical Marxist-feminist deconstructionist"; her essay "Can the Subaltern Speak?" is a core text in postcolonial theory. Other major works include her translation and editing of Jacques Derrida's *Of Grammatology* (1976), *In Other Worlds: Essays in Cultural Politics* (1987), *Selected Subaltern Studies* (1988), *The Post-Colonial Critics* (1990), *Outside in the Teaching Machine* (1993), *A Critique of Postcolonial Reason: Towards a History of the Vanishing Present* (1999), *Death of a Discipline* (2003), and *Other Asias* (2005).

Todorov, Tzvetan

Bulgarian-born literary theorist and cultural critic (1939–), whose works focus on the fantastic and the extreme. Major works translated into English include *The Fantastic: A Structural Approach to a Literary Genre* (1973), *Conquest of America: The Question of the Other* (1984), *Mikhail Bakhtin: The Dialogic Principle* (1984), *On Human Diversity* (1993), *Voices from the Gulag: Life and*

Death in Communist Bulgaria (1999), *Facing the Extreme: Moral Life in the Concentration Camps* (2000), *Imperfect Garden: The Legacy of Humanism* (2002), *Hope and Memory: Lessons from the Twentieth Century* (2003), *In Defense of the Enlightenment* (2009), and *The Fear of Barbarians: Beyond the Clash of Civilizations* (2010).

White, Hayden

American historian and cultural critic (1928–) who developed poststructuralist "metahistory." Major works include *Metahistory: The Historical Imagination in Nineteenth-Century Europe* (1973), *Tropics of Discourse: Essays in Cultural Criticism* (1978), *The Content of the Form: Narrative Discourse and Historical Representation* (1987), *Figural Realism: Studies in the Mimesis Effect* (1999), and *The Fiction of Narrative: Essays on History, Literature, and Theory, 1957–2007* (2010).

Žižek, Slavoj

Žižek (1949–) is a Slovenian continental philosopher and critical theorist in the tradition of Hegel, Marx, and Lacan. He studied psychoanalysis at the University of Paris VIII Vincennes, and is considered the chief contemporary "heir" of Jacques Lacan. He calls himself an "antipoststructuralist," who objects to the "obscurantism" of poststructuralist writings. His major works in English include *The Sublime Object of Ideology* (1989), *Looking Awry: An Introduction to Lacan Through Popular Culture* (1991), *Enjoy Your Symptom! Jacques Lacan in Hollywood* (1992), *The Ticklish Subject* (1999), *Interrogating the Real* (2005), *How to Read Lacan* (2006), *The Parallax View* (2006), *In Defense of Lost Causes* (2008), *Violence: Six Sideways Reflections* (2008), *First as Tragedy, Then as Farce* (2009), and *Living in the End Times* (2010).

Important Works

Useful guidebooks for beginners

Barry, Peter. *Beginning Theory: An Introduction to Literary and Cultural Theory* (3rd edn). Manchester University Press, 2009.

This book makes an excellent textbook for undergraduate classes in literary theory. Barry does a good job explaining the fundamental ideas of a variety of theories, and gives accessible examples without overwhelming the beginning student.

Bertens, Hans. *Literary Theory: The Basics* (2nd edn). Routledge, 2007.

As the title suggests, this book covers "the basics," providing a clear and concise overview of the main types and ideas of literary theory. It is an excellent starting point for beginners, and the second edition updates the coverage of theories with the inclusion of theories of sexuality and ecocriticism.

Bressler, Charles. *Literary Criticism: An Introduction to Theory and Practice* (5th edn). Prentice Hall, 2011.

Bressler takes a broad approach combining the traditional approaches to "literary criticism" with the more contemporary insights of "literary theory." This is a good comprehensive look at thirteen major schools of twentieth-century literary thought. It is a useful beginning-level textbook designed to help students begin to write clearly and critically about literature; it does not go into much depth about the philosophical or political aspects of literary theory.

Culler, Jonathan. *Literary Theory: A Very Short Introduction* (2nd edn). Oxford University Press, 2011.

Culler's book is, as the title says, a very short introduction, and a very good starting point. He gives clear explanations of the philosophies that underlie types of theory without being overly pedantic. This second edition covers up-to-date developments in literary theory, including ecocriticism and the "death" of theory. Culler asks excellent questions about the relationship between literature and culture, and gives clear accessible examples of ways that various types of theory illuminate a literary text. This book is part of a series of *Very Short Introductions* on a wide variety of topics, including modernism, Marxism, Foucault, and postmodernism, all written by renowned scholars in the field.

Eagleton, Terry. *Literary Theory: An Introduction* (3rd edn). **University of Minnesota Press, 2008.**

Eagleton wrote one of the first "guides" to literary theory in the early 1980s, and this third edition has kept up to date with major developments since then. His book is particularly good in discussing the history of "English" literary studies. His discussions of the philosophies that underlie literary theory, such as phenomenology, can be very dense and daunting to beginners; his explanation of Marxist theories is outstanding. His references are oriented largely toward canonical British literature.

Hall, Donald. *Literary and Cultural Theory: From Basic Principles to Advanced Applications.* **Houghton Mifflin, 2000.**

This is a good textbook for a course on literary theory. Hall explains ten types of literary theory, from New Criticism to New Historicism; his selections of theory are somewhat dated and limited. The main strength of the book is the inclusion of critical essays, each by a different renowned scholar, illuminating the application of a type of theory to a specific well-known literary text.

Klages, Mary. *Literary Theory: A Guide for the Perplexed.* **Continuum Press, 2006.**

In my opinion, this is the best guide available!

Ryan, Michael. *Literary Theory: A Practical Introduction* (2nd edn). **Wiley-Blackwell, 2007.**

This book is designed to be a companion volume to Julie Rivkin and Michael Ryan's *Literary Theory: An Anthology*; it provides clear and detailed explanations of a wide variety of theories, and can be used by itself to provide beginning students with thorough coverage of up-to-date developments in literary and cultural theory. It gives practical examples of how to read various literary texts through the lenses of different theories.

Sarup, Madan. *An Introductory Guide to Poststructuralism and Postmodernism* (2nd edn). University of Georgia Press, 1993.

This is an outstanding guide to many of the most important post-structuralist theories, though it is somewhat out of date in terms of twenty-first century theories. Sarup's explanations of Lacan and of Lyotard are particularly clear and useful.

Tyson, Lois. *Critical Theory Today: A User-Friendly Guide* (2nd edn). Routledge, 2006.

This is an excellent textbook, an overview of a wide variety of types of theory. Tyson illustrates her explanations of theories with reference to popular culture and to well-known canonical literary texts; throughout the book she uses F. Scott Fitzgerald's *The Great Gatsby* as a central reference, showing how each type of theory provides a lens for viewing the text. This book also has useful questions that help students learn to use the theories for reading other literary texts on their own.

Other good guides for beginners

There are also many books designed for beginning students that address specific types of theories and provide excellent accessible but not simplistic explanations of the foundations, principles, and problems of each type.

The *For Beginners* series is my personal favorite. These books are in graphic format, created by knowledgeable teams of writers and illustrators. They make learning theory as fun as reading a comic book or manga novel, and all are accessible and informative. If not otherwise listed, the publisher for all of these is "For Beginners." The series includes:

W. Terrence Gordon, *Saussure for Beginners*, 1996.
Richard Appignanesi, *Freud for Beginners*, Pantheon 2003.
Rius, *Marx for Beginners,* Pantheon, 2003.
Jim Powell and Van Howell, *Derrida for Beginners*, 2007.
Lydia Alix Fillingham, *Foucault for Beginners*, 2007.

Marc Sautet, *Nietzsche for Beginners*, 2007.
Richard Osborne, *Philosophy for Beginners*, 2007.
Robert Cavalier, *Plato for Beginners*, 2007.
Jim Powell, *Postmodernism for Beginners*, 2007.
Donald Palmer, *Structuralism and Poststructuralism for Beginners*, 2007.
Jim Powell, *Deconstruction for Beginners*, 2008.
W. Terrence Gordon, *Linguistics for Beginners*, 2008.
Phillip Hill, *Lacan for Beginners*, 2009.

The *Introducing* series is another set of beginner's guides in graphic format. All of these are published by Totem Books, unless otherwise indicated. The series includes:

Richard Appignanesi, *Introducing Postmodernism: A Graphic Guide to Cutting Edge Thinking*, 2003.
Stuart Sim, *Introducing Critical Theory: A Graphic Guide*, 3rd edn, 2005.
Chris Horrocks, *Introducing Foucault: A Graphic Guide*, 4th edn, 2005.
R. L. Trask, *Introducing Linguistics*, 3rd edn, 2005.
Rupert Woodfin, *Introducing Marxism: A Graphic Guide*, 2nd edn, 2005.
Chris Rodrigues, *Introducing Modernism: A Graphic Guide*, 3rd edn, 2006.
Dave Robinson, *Introducing Philosophy: A Graphic Guide*, 2007.
Darian Leader, *Introducing Lacan: A Graphic Guide reprint*, 2010.
Paul Cobley, *Introducing Semiotics: A Graphic Guide*, 2010.
Ziauddin Sardar, *Introducing Cultural Studies: A Graphic Guide*, reprint 2010.
Cathia Jenainati, *Introducing Feminism: A Graphic Guide*, 2010.

Another great series for beginning theory students is *Very Short Introductions*. These are written in traditional format and provide thorough coverage of a particular type of theory. All are published by Oxford University Press unless otherwise noted. The series includes:

Jonathan Culler, *Literary Theory: A Very Short Introduction*, 2000.
Simon Critchley, *Continental Philosophy: A Very Short Introduction*, 2001.

Anthony Storr, *Freud: A Very Short Introduction*, 2001.
Peter Singer, *Marx: A Very Short Introduction*, 2001.
Michael Tanner, *Nietzsche: A Very Short Introduction*, 2001.
Jonathan Culler, *Barthes: A Very Short Introduction*, 2002.
Edward Craig, *Philosophy: A Very Short Introduction*, 2002.
Catherine Belsey, *Poststructuralism: A Very Short Introduction*, 2002.
P. H. Matthews, *Linguistics: A Very Short Introduction*, 2003.
Julia Annas, *Plato: A Very Short Introduction*, 2003.
Christopher Butler, *Postmodernism: A Very Short Introduction*, 2003.
Robert J. C. Young, *Postcolonialism: A Very Short Introduction*, 2003.
Gary Gutting, *Foucault: A Very Short Introduction*, 2005.
Margaret Walters, *Feminism: A Very Short Introduction*, 2006.
Véronique Mottier, *Sexuality: A Very Short Introduction*, 2008.
Christopher Butler, *Modernism: A Very Short Introduction*, 2010.
Stephen Bronner, *Critical Theory: A Very Short Introduction*, 2011.
Stephen Law, *Humanism: A Very Short Introduction*, 2011.

Anthologies

These are collections of pieces by major theorists, containing the most important essays or excerpts from longer works of each. Such anthologies are often used as textbooks in an introductory or intermediate literary theory course. The essays contained in these anthologies are primary sources from theorists, and as such are often dense and complicated to read on their own. While most anthologies include a wide selection of original texts, some are more comprehensive or up to date than others.

Julie Rivkin and Michael Ryan, eds. *Literary Theory: An Anthology* (3rd edn). Wiley-Blackwell, 2004.

In my opinion, this is probably the best anthology for students of literary theory; it is inclusive and representative.

Vincent Leitch, William Cain, Laurie Finke, Barbara Johnson, John McGowan, T. Denean Sharpley-Whiting, and Jeffrey Williams, eds. *The Norton Anthology of Theory and Criticism* (2nd edn). W.W. Norton, 2010.

This is one of the most up-to-date and comprehensive anthologies, containing almost 3,000 pages of essays representing twentieth-century theories, non-Western theories, and theorists of "theory."

Hazard Adams and Leroy Searle, eds. *Critical Theory Since 1965.* University Press of Florida, 1985.

This textbook contains the major essays of important theorists up to 1985, its year of publication. The essays are well selected but presented in an almost random order. It's a good book, but needs updating. Its companion volume, *Critical Theory Since Plato*, contains a great collection of the essays and theorists who provided the foundations for later critical theory.

Daphne Patai, *Theory's Empire: An Anthology of Dissent.* Columbia University Press, 2005.

This anthology contains a powerful variety of essays arguing about and criticizing what has become orthodoxy and dogma in literary and cultural theory. It would be most useful to advanced students of theory who want to engage in current debates about the usefulness and status of "theory."

Books for beginners on individual theorists and theories

There are hundreds of books out there explaining individual theorists and types of theory; the ones listed below are the most accessible for beginning theory students. All provide a thorough overview of the field, a reading guide for a theorist or theory's most important works, and an extensive bibliography for further reading.

I recommend the series entitled *Routledge Critical Thinkers*. These are sophisticated and complete explanations of the major thinkers and theorists encountered in beginning and advanced literary theory. They are both accessible and challenging, and will lead beginners to the next level. All of these are published by Routledge. The series includes:

Adam Roberts, *Frederic Jameson*, 2000.
Claire Colebrook, *Gilles Deleuze*, 2001.
Sarah Salih, *Judith Butler*, 2001.

Martin McQuillan, *Paul de Man*, 2001.
Stephen Morton, *Gayatri Chakravorty Spivak*, 2002.
Simon Malpas, *Jean-François Lyotard*, 2002.
Lee Spinks, *Friedrich Nietzsche*, 2003.
Nicholas Royle, *Jacques Derrida*, 2003.
Noëlle McAfee, *Julia Kristeva*, 2003.
Karl Sims, *Paul Ricoeur*, 2003.
Graham Allen, *Roland Barthes*, 2003.
Tony Myers, *Slavoj Žižek*, 2003.
Sean Homer, *Jacques Lacan*, 2005.
David Huddart, *Homi Bhaba*, 2006.
Luke Ferretter, *Jacques Lacan*, 2006.
Ross Wilson, *Theodor Adorno*, 2007.
Bill Ashcroft and Pal Ahluwahlia, *Edward Said*, 2008.
Richard Lane, *Jean Baudrillard*, 2009.
Alaistair Renfrew, *Mikhail Bakhtin*, 2009.
Pamela Thurschwell, *Sigmund Freud*, 2009.

LIST OF KEY TERMS

Word list

LIST OF
MAJOR FIGURES

INDEX